GAMIFICATION

by

Chris Collins

"You can discover more about a person in an hour of play than in a year of conversation."
— Plato

CONTENTS

THE HACK

Give me a lever long enough and a fulcrum on which to place it, and I shall move the world. - Archimedes

Sooner or later in business we all need to move a mountain. It doesn't matter whether you own or manage a sandwich shop, car dealership, tech start-up, or a big sales team. Maybe you have to dramatically increase sales, profit margins, improve turnover, or launch a new product. These tasks can seem like mountains. And at some point in your business, you will have to move them.

One thing I know to be true: you can't move a mountain alone. You need support. And the more committed your support team is, the stronger you will be.

While researching this book, I was astounded to learn that over half of America's workforce today is unhappy with their jobs.[1] And according to a Gallup Poll, that percentage swung as high as eighty-five percent.[2]

Let that sink in.

It's an uncomfortable truth to hear, to know that odds are that at some point at least half of your employees have been unhappy with their jobs. If you're going to move a mountain, you want the best support you can have. You want devotion, the kind of dedicated, gung-ho workers who build the pyramids (believe it or not, they were built by volunteers, not slaves). But how do you get this kind of team?

The answer is *Gamification*.

Now do me a favor and picture your business, or any business, as a machine. A physical, real world machine. Let's say an internal combustion engine in a car.

The car takes in fuel from the pump. The intake valve opens, and the piston moves down so that the cylinder fills with a mixture of air and gasoline. The piston pulls back to compress the mixture, the spark plug emits a spark, and the mixture explodes, releasing the energy that propels the piston down and, in short, makes the car move.

Guess what? This is not an efficient machine. And the business that it represents is not an efficient business.

Why?

Because creation of the energy that drives the car is dependent on fuel, a finite and often expensive external resource. For a business, that energy is the bottom line that drives the value of the company. And the fuel is the employees.

Unfortunately for cars and other physical, real-world machines, efficiency hasn't yet moved beyond producing less energy than taken in. Eventually all machines break down as a result of this.

But in this book I will show you how by implementing a simple, common sense life-hack into your work environment, a system called Gamification, you can create a machine whose fuel source yields energy at maximum efficiency. Your machine will function as close to perpetual motion as possible, building momentum so powerful you will become an unstoppable force.

All you need to create this machine is to follow the system I lay out in this book. Gamification is your hack to improving sales, profits, morale, consistency, and overall fun.

Gamification is using game thinking or strategy in non-game, real world settings to problem solve or increase user contributions.

In this case that means building teams and having the enthusiastic, happy, and driven employees essential to a sustainable, healthy business.

Maybe you're skeptical. Maybe you think games are for children, or you don't like games, or you aren't good at games. I've heard many business owners and sales managers start out saying and feeling those same things, and then witnessed firsthand as they went on to double their sales, increase margins and profits, and launch new, more profitable income streams, all while their employees were laughing, high-fiving, and racing to get to work. They were able to create perpetual motion.

Let me explain further: Your employees' energy is something your customers can feel.

Think about going to the DMV. What do you feel when faced with a frowning, disinterested worker who tells you to take a number and wait? You probably don't feel very good. In psychology, this is called mirroring. You subconsciously assume the behavior and attitude of the person you're interacting with.

Now imagine a DMV where all of the employees are smiling and having the best day of their lives. I know, I know, government employees happy? *Yeah right!* But we're suspending disbelief here.

Today the employees at the DMV are working hard, they're happy, and they're even friendly to you. Subconsciously you reflect that attitude. That's how we're designed to function as human beings. Suddenly waiting doesn't seem so bad.

What this means is that when your team is having fun, and is driven and challenged, your customers will feel it. Energy is contagious. When your employees feel good, your customers feel good, and when they feel good, they buy more, your income grows, and you feel even better.

You're going to create a new culture in your office or business. The positive energy instilled in your staff through Gamification will be infectious, and before long everyone will be buzzing with competitive spirit, coaching and cheering each other on.

When you successfully increase the morale of your staff, their confidence, discipline, and willingness to perform will grow. Studies have proven time and again that employees who are happier perform and communicate better. When you can create the kind of positive, recognition-based environment Gamification fosters, you'll increase productivity and overall sales.

As a leader, whether manager or company owner, your work culture will be one people love being a part of, where employees constantly push themselves to improve, because through Gamification gives them a personal investment in their work performance. And since their wins are your wins, you'll find your company gaining momentum.

As this happens, you'll very likely need to take on more employees to continue to meet demand. This is where the winning culture you've created comes in. Winners are attracted to winners. When you're winning and your employees are winning, word will get out that your workplace is one for winners.

Inevitably, like dogs to a bone, the best of the best talent, or what I call "Top Dogs" will come sniffing around, barking at your door, wanting to work in the fun, exciting, and *winning* environment you've created.

A University of Toronto study referenced on the Business Insider website showed that department output increases by 54% when a new top dog arrives.[3] Even if the top dog leaves, studies show the department *still retains* a 48% increase in performance afterward.[4] And that's assuming they ever leave. Because not only will your culture attract these top dogs, but it will give you a much better chance to keep them.

Countless times, I've seen a business with low morale, high

turnover, and a bad reputation become a powerhouse, turning its destiny and financial situation around overnight.

These businesses end up with happier employees, more customers, and lower turnover. They attract the top dogs. They make more money. And most of all, they can move mountains.

Now you can start making all of this happen tomorrow through a simple hack, a system called gamification.

IT'S HAPPENING RIGHT UNDER YOUR NOSE

"There is nothing more deceptive than an obvious fact."
— Arthur Conan Doyle

Gamification is a hack that will enable you to quickly become the leader you need to be to move mountains. But this isn't magic or any kind of trick. This is a system founded on common sense, and a product of the fundamental human desire for happiness and challenges in life. It already exists all around us.

Years ago, when Starbucks launched a new product, VIA Instant Coffee, they faced a major consumer perception problem right away.

Instant coffee, as far as most people were concerned, wasn't as good as the real thing. It was something astronauts might use in space, or something for that guy rushing so quickly out the door he doesn't even have time to brew a real cup. But it wasn't the real thing. I definitely never found myself waking up, thinking: *Man, I could really go for a cup of instant coffee right now.*

That perception was a major hurdle for Starbucks. It didn't matter that they had developed a new process to create a better cup of instant coffee, one nearly indistinguishable from the real thing, not to mention quicker and easier to make. People still believed that instant coffee was inferior coffee.

Starbucks is a massive corporation, with over 21,000 franchises all around the world. Obviously, this kind of presence naturally gives a company a huge leg up when trying to launch a new product. Still, you don't have to look any further than the failure of New Coke to also see how colossally a new product can fail even for such a massive company.

Comparatively speaking, a small company might face a greater risk with a new product, including loss of jobs or even the demise the company itself, but while a Starbucks-sized company might not face complete demise, failure of a new product like VIA could have resulted in significant job losses, stock devaluation, and sent a shockwave through corporate America itself.

That's a big risk. Especially on a product with such negative preconceptions surrounding.

So how did Starbucks make it VIA such a success?

To start, they put it up front, right by the register in every store. That made sense. But putting it in front of the customers, even with advertising, wasn't enough. What Starbucks did next was brilliant.

They Gamified it.

Around the time VIA came out, I liked to go to Starbucks every day for my morning cup of black coffee. At first, I noticed VIA placed at the counter, but I didn't think much more of it more than a curious, *what's that?*

As I went to pay for my coffee, the barista asked if I wanted to purchase a box of a VIA. She asked with a smile that wasn't the kind you'd expect on a person who dragged herself out of bed at four a.m. to go to work, but simply a genuine smile. I hadn't even had my coffee yet for the day. But that smile hit me like a jolt of caffeine. I felt myself smile back. Then she told me that VIA was better than the usual instant coffee, and you know what? I believed her.

As I continued going to this Starbucks over the next few weeks, the workers would always ask me if I wanted a box of VIA with my morning coffee. They never missed an opportunity to ask, and they had a similar positive attitude, like they were really into this product, that they cared about whether I bought it.

One day I was on my way to meet a client and I stopped at a different Starbucks to get coffee for us. Without missing a beat, the barista smiled and asked if I wanted a box of *guess what?* VIA instant coffee.

As I waited for the coffees, I noticed a dry erase board in the back room. Curious, I peered around the corner to see what was written on it. What I saw shocked me. It said something to the effect of:

"Top Store In The Market For VIA Sales This Month Wins A Night Out To A Restaurant Of Its Choosing."

Genius! I thought. Such a simple incentive, but it was working. Since VIA had been released, I had yet to buy a single cup of coffee without being asked if I wanted to take a box of it with me.

I bought VIA several times. Starbucks had sold me. Not just through its ad campaign and by putting VIA front of me, but by overriding my preconceptions about instant coffee through the positive energy of the employees selling it to me, energy instilled in them through Gamification, with nothing more at stake than a night out to dinner.

This is Gamification in its simplest form.

It seems obvious in hindsight, but you'd be amazed by how many businesses overlook the obvious. Not Starbucks, though. They had launched a potentially risky new product, banking unfathomable amounts of money on its success, and the foundation of their strategy to sell it was based on a game.

If you know how to look for them, you'll find games in all kinds of businesses. Think of that time you bought a new pair of athletic shoes, and the salesperson offered you the chance to upgrade your insoles or get water protection.

Without a doubt, they were playing a game behind the scenes. Most likely, the company offered a spiff (incentive) for each up-sell, and I'd bet the Top Dog each month also won a free pair of shoes of his choice.

You even see Gamification within games. It is definitely not the NFL's proudest moment, but a major reason the New Orleans Saints won the 2009 Super Bowl was because the team's coaches offered players cash prizes for big plays, big hits, and even injuring opposing players.

Now I don't support violence of that sort in any way. But this speaks to the power of Gamification. Starters and rotation players on a Super Bowl caliber team earn millions of dollars a year. Relatively speaking, the cash prizes they got as bounties for big plays were peanuts. What's a one thousand dollar spiff against hundreds of thousands of dollars per game? Nothing, right?

But they weren't nothing, because these small spiffs were what spurred peer pressure in the locker room between the individuals on the team, to perform better, win more bounties, and this led to the Saints winning the Lombardi Trophy.

I can't stress enough that it's always important to play within the rules. The Saints broke the rules and were punished; however, that doesn't take away from this as an example of how much influence the even small stakes and minor competitions of games can have on employees. Since that season, the bounties have stopped, and the Saints have yet to come close to winning another Super Bowl.

I see Gamification everywhere. After you start playing games with your team, you will too.

You'll notice it in other businesses. You'll see that energy is higher in businesses that play games, the employees are more attentive, and more connected and invested in their jobs than normal. You'll even start noticing products that are Gamified, just by how they are presented to you. When you notice these games, don't be afraid to seek out the manager and share ideas. I've learned a lot by doing this.

By the end of this year (2015), over 50% of companies will have Gamified at least some aspect of their businesses. Already, 70% of Global 2000 companies (such as eBay and Amazon), have at least one Gamified aspect of their business, ranging from games on their websites to employee training.[5]

Like I said, Gamification is all around you. Big companies like those above have nearly endless funds to devote to figuring out ways to increase revenue, and this is one major system they've chosen to implement.

Now it's up to you whether you want to join them.

THE BREAKTHROUGH

Give me a deck of cards and a fist full of cash and I'll increase your sales, employee morale, and anything else you need in your business. - Chris Collins

One hot summer day in Los Angeles, a close friend of mine was dead center of a huge boom.

This boom was just like the Gold Rush of the 1800s, and he was selling the shovels!

He was in the perfect position to provide a huge service to a growing industry.

He owned a company that sold the fertilizer that literally could grow any fruit or vegetable bigger than God ever intended.

At the same time, cannabis was becoming legal in certain states, and this created a need/demand for his product.

With his products, cannabis growers could dramatically increase yields per plant in a legal climate where federal laws conflicted with state laws, and limited growers of cannabis to ninety-nine plants before facing federal prosecution. So growers needed every advantage in increasing the size or yields of each plant they grew, because they couldn't grow more than ninety-nine plants without facing jail time, or at minimum, costly legal issues.

My friend is one of the smartest marketers and business talents I know, and was navigating huge growth and a changing market like a master.

On this day, the Los Angeles Convention center was having a Hemp Fest, a.k.a. a convention for cannabis, and he had stepped up big time.

He wanted to use this opportunity to make a big splash and a capture a bigger piece of this market. So he had set himself up as the anchor of the convention. His booth was straight center in the back of the convention hall, with eight huge pillars going up, maybe 35 feet. On either side of his booth, he had two Hummer SUV's wrapped in vinyl displaying his company name.

With his marketing savvy and experience, he knew how to create a presence that not only couldn't be ignored, but made you want to check it out from any point in the convention hall. He had successfully hijacked attention from the hundreds of other businesses at this event, which was exactly what he had set out to do.

I believe he told me the space and set-up cost him over two hundred thousand dollars. On top of that, he had flown down his sales staff from Canada, plus a few independent contractors from around the country. In total, he had twelve people working the floor.

He had invited me and another friend from our mastermind group to come support him and check out what he was doing.

I had just purchased booth space at the upcoming National Auto Convention, and was a virgin to conventions myself, so I was really interested in learning how to make an impact and stand out in a big convention environment.

The first thing I noticed was the a huge crowd he had at his booth. People were crammed in like sardines.

After walking around and meeting his team, we went back to a VIP lounge and sat down to talk about the event. I asked him what his target was, considering the huge investment he made and the effort he took to get his entire team out here for the show. What would he measure to determine whether the convention was a success?

He explained that even though the convention would pull in mostly recreational smokers, his real target was the hydroponic shop owners who worked directly with growers. His goal was to engage them and build a list to market to after the event.

My next question was obvious to me, but caught him off-guard. "So how many store owners have you gotten info on so far today?" I said.

He looked me straight in the eye and said, "I should know that, I know, but I don't."

"Is your team competitive?" I asked.

"Oh yeah," he said.

"Well then do you want to have some fun with this and collect a bunch of hydro shop owners info over the next two days?"

"How do we do that?" he said.

"I bet if you could get your hands on the new iPhone that just came out, we could hold a contest for it among your staff working the floor. Whoever collects the most business cards or customer contact info wins the iPhone."

I knew that getting a new iPhone was a bit of a stretch, because it had just been released a few days before, and was already sold out everywhere. It was being hyped all over the national news. People who were able to get their hands on these phones were selling them for huge profits on eBay.

My friend quickly went to work, and we got lucky. Within a few hours, the concierge at the Peninsula Hotel in Beverly Hills, where he was staying, had done the impossible and gotten their hands on not one, but two new iPhones.

Next, we had someone from his staff create and print hundreds of short customer data sheets for the staff to use to collect contact info in the absence of a hydroponic shop owner having a business card.

First thing the following morning, before the convention doors opened, surrounded in a big circle by his sales team, I did my best to channel Alec Baldwin's sales speech from *Glengarry Glen Ross,* minus the whole "third place you're fired" part.

"So, we want to have some fun, and my friend Chris here has an idea," my friend said.

I held up one of the iPhones still in the box, and waved it around.

"Anyone know what this is?"

Their eyes lit up.

We handed out a simple one-sheet detailing the game. The person to collect the most hydroponic shop owners contact information would win a new iPhone. Second place would win a set of steak knives or $200, and third place would win $100.

By now, the team was buzzing and shifting back and forth like caged tigers made to stand still. A couple of them pushed each other in a friendly way, but sending a clear message that the iPhone was theirs.

I had met his top sales person the day before, and while everyone was watching me, I walked across the circle, held out an iPhone, and said: "Should I just give this to you now, or are you going to take it easy today?"

The rest of the team went *nuts.*

"Whoaaa! Hand that over here," one said.

"That's not right," another yelled out.

As I turned around and walked back, my friend and I looked at each other and laughed. We had them! This was going to be fun.

We closed by telling the team that the contest restarts each day, giving them a new chance to win an iPhone. To get them going for the first two hours of the convention, each business card collected counted as double.

"Now let's have some fun and make some friends today," my friend said.

Then the meeting broke, and the team bounced around, talking and laughing as the convention doors opened, letting in the crowd.

If my memory serves me correctly, the winner of our game that day collected seventy-eight business cards, and the person in second-place collected seventy-one. In total, the team collected the names, business names, addresses and phone numbers of well over a thousand hydroponics shop owners.

Best of all, the team had a blast. It seemed less like work and more like kids playing on a schoolyard, and my friend had tangible results for his investment.

The day that happened, I realized that what I had been doing in the car industry for years—using games to motivate a team—could apply to any industry or environment where employees interacted with customers.

Notice I didn't say sales environment, because sometimes you just want to build a list of specific customer profile questions of a target market, or collect customer data. By using this system I am going to share, you can turn non-hunting dogs into hunters.

I have yet to find a limit to the application of Gamification. A recent review of twenty-four scholarly articles found that Gamification increases attitude, motivation, and enjoyment in employees across the board, whether it was kids studying for a spelling bee or adults learning a new computer task on Microsoft Office via a talking paper clip.[6]

It does this by bringing your team closer together and helping spread new ideas. The mix of competition and the social aspects of it are what drive people to want to do better, but it also makes them feel better too.

Currently 40% of the top 1000 companies by market use Gamification techniques as their primary mechanism for business operations. The Gamification industry itself is on pace to easily exceed five billion dollars within the next few years. You read that right. *Billion*, with a big, fat *holy-cow-that's-a-ton-of-money-B*.[7]

This is happening because Gamification works. But for it to work, it requires a leader who is committed to it, and who from the start buys into it as his or her course of action.

From there, all it takes is a goal, i.e. a clear idea of what you want to achieve, **and a prize**. Then stir the pot, sit back, and watch the fun.

THE MOUNTAIN

"When you reach the top of the mountain, keep climbing."
– Famous Zen Buddhist Saying

What the above saying means to me is that a journey never ends. As a business grows, fights ,and claws to succeed, yes, it will have to move metaphorical mountains, but the overall journey is more like climbing one.

Facebook, Google, Apple, etc.: these companies are all at the top of their respective fields, but they continue to innovate and climb higher every day because the mountain each of them is climbing continues to rise. Even as success comes, challenges remain, and so does the need to continue climbing.

If you're reading this book, my assumption is that you're either not yet at the top of the mountain or else looking for a slight edge. And if you happen to be there, well, then you know already that there is no end to the climb. Wherever you are, you're on the mountain, and from here on, Gamification will be the wind at your back, pushing you higher.

* * *

Since the dawn of civilization, individuals and teams have been pushed to the highest levels of success by one fundamental human element: *desire*. Call it want, wish, demand, lust, or whatever you like, from the desire for a kingdom to the simple desire for another breath, desire is what moves people.

In a paper in 1943, the psychologist Abraham Maslow described what is now famously known as Maslow's hierarchy of needs, and which to this day remains an essential framework of many management strategies. Maslow formed a pyramid of these needs (image below), much like the food pyramid you've probably seen a million times

Physiological, Safety, Love/belonging, Esteem and Self-Actualization; he called these our human needs. But the way I see them, only the bottom row, the physiological, represents our true needs, the physical requirements of life—air, food, water, shelter, and clothing—and even those are tethered to the rest as focal points of our desires, because it's our nature to want the best air, food, water, shelter and clothing we can have.

As for the other four: we don't need them so much as we desire them. We want professional and personal security, want connections to others and recognition, want self-esteem, and most of all want to make the most of our lives.

Gamification works because it incorporates these fundamental desires into a single motivational stratagem for the workplace.

Through competition, social interaction, and achievement, Gamification fulfills the desires of its players within the work environment. It improves job security, encourages teamwork and connection, provides instant and long-term validation, and allows people to reach their true potential. On top of that, when the momentum really gets going, and the money is flowing in, Gamification hits the bottom row most of all, as your employees and ultimately you end up with the best air, food, water, shelter and clothing possible.

None of the above is new information, but only recently has Gamification really come into the workplace and changed the way we interact with our employees.

Capitalization on basic human desires and needs has always produced the strongest results. As I said earlier, the Great Pyramid wasn't built by slaves. That's a fallacy. It was built by workers who wanted to build it. Likewise, the greatest armies weren't comprised solely by conscripted soldiers, but by ones who wanted to fight and win. Look no further back in history than World War II. By the end, the German Army was made up mostly of men too young or too old to fight, and who didn't want to be there anyway. But our soldiers, along with the allied forces, they couldn't be turned away. My own grandfather was so drawn to serving to his country that he lied about his age and joined the Navy at seventeen, when the required age was eighteen. He wanted to serve his country even if it meant paying the ultimate price. Like the rest of our service members. They were moved by their desire, to win, to preserve their freedom, and to protect their families and brethren in arms. And they won.

Now, so will you.

The recent shift towards Gamification has come about very much due to the younger generation entering the workforce, primarily millennials.

Whereas previous generations often functioned with a mentality to clock in and clock out, and work hard to provide a better life for their children—and that's what they did—millennials have grown up inundated with the notion that they deserve more than clocking in and clocking out, and that their personal desires, often to contribute and be a part of a bigger cause, are what is most important. Recent research has shown that, in 18-29 year olds, 79% said that enjoying their job was more important than making big money.[8]

Some people shun millennials for this mentality. I see no benefit in complaining about it, though, but huge leverage in embracing it. As Polonius says to Hamlet, "This above all: to thine own self be true." No matter who you serve, you serve yourself first.

I'm not advocating selfishness. What I'm saying is that no matter how noble or good we strive to be, our desires even to do the most selfless things ultimately stem from purely within ourselves. Millennials, more than any previous generation, embody the truth, that we are all vessels of our own desire. Since I've established that desire drives success, it's your job as an employer to create the desires that inspire and drive your employees. If almost 80% of young employees value fun above money, then giving them fun should be a no-brainer.

In the preceding chapters, I explained Gamification macroscopically in the hope of conveying the broad scope of its application. But now you're ready to start using it, and it's time to zoom in on the nuts and bolts of the system.

First I'm going to explain how to set up Gamification, as well as the different elements of it. From there, I'll detail some of the best games I've found for creating the fun and competitive work environments essential to building momentum and yielding positive, impactful results.

STACKING THE DECK

Earlier in this book, I mentioned that all you need to implement this system is a goal and a prize. That seems simple enough. And guess what? It is.

In our universe, most things connect or operate in the most economical way possible. In science, this is called the Principle of Parsimony. So if all you need is a goal and a prize, then you must be ready to start, right?

So what game will you play? Why do you think that game will work? What kind of prize will you offer? Why that prize? Is it good enough? Will everyone want to play this game? What will you do if some employees don't want to play? What's your plan for the next game? For the next year of games? For the next five years of games? How are you going to keep these games going indefinitely and ensure that your employees remain enthusiastic and driven enough to meet the demands of your industry?

The questions come quickly, don't they?

My goal isn't just to tell you what to do and give you answers to questions, but to prepare you to both implement this system and fully understand how and why it works, so that when you're faced with questions or issues, you will be the expert, and you will know what to do.

Everything starts with a goal and a prize.

While these two concepts overlap, especially when an employee or team is working hard to win a prize, which represents a goal for them, it's important to recognize the difference between these concepts in this system.

The *goal* is what you desire from your employees, in short, whatever you want to have a positive impact on your business. Your goal can be collecting business cards, quicker turnaround times, selling more of a product, or anything else. The reality is that this goal benefits you much more than your employees. Sure, they'll reap some rewards if you reach it, but they have their own desires, and this business is not their business, or else this department is not their department, and the end result of the goal is yours.

The *prize* is what motivates your employees. Whether it's cash, a new TV, even a car, or something as basic as a gold star or employee of the month plaque, the prize is separate from your goal and exists purely for your employees. Recognizing and understanding that this is what drives your employees within this system is what allows you to capitalize on their efforts. Got it? Good.

Then you're ready to get started.

I like to call creating a game "Stacking the Deck." If you've played cards before, you'll recognize this as a term for arranging the cards so that they land in your favor, and you increase your odds of winning. Obviously in a card game this constitutes cheating, but in business, through Gamification, this is a perfectly viable, non-cheating approach to moving the odds of success into your favor.

I've created a series of ten steps to help you stack your deck.

1. ESTABLISH YOUR GOAL

The first step you have to take to stack the deck is to choose your goal. In reality, this is going to have to come from you and what you want your employees to do to benefit your business, but for the purpose of this explanation, I'm going to create an example. From here on in this part of the book, consider yourself the proud owner of one location in a national submarine sandwich chain called *Bulldog Subs*.

Bear in mind that this Bulldog Subs franchise is your only business. In fact, it's your lifeblood. And right now it's performing just well enough for you to pay the bills and get by. It's average.

But you want more than average. Maybe this means taking in more income so that you can buy that new car, or pay for your child's education, or finance another franchise. Maybe you want recognition for owning one the best Bulldog Subs franchises in the country. Or maybe you just want to ensure long-term stability. Whatever your aim is, it is the foundation of your goal for every game when you use this system. And today that goal is to increase the income your Bulldog Subs takes in.

So now you need to identify an area of your business where you can increase income immediately and sustainably.

2. CHOOSE YOUR MVP

You're probably familiar with the term MVP from sports, as an acronym for Most Valuable Player. But that's not the MVP you're looking for in your business. Your MVP is more than any player and more than any team. Your MVP is your means of reaching your goal. It is your *Most Valuable Product*.

The MVP is the product that you're going to focus on with your games.

To be clear, your MVP doesn't actually have to be a product at all. It could be business cards from hydroponic shop owners, positive comments on your Yelp page, or even high fives on the youth basketball team you coach. You don't even have to have one MVP. I've seen businesses with two, three, four, and sometimes even more MVPs. Working as a service advisor, I often found we had multiple MVPs, with all the different upsells we could provide to customers. The key to finding your MVP(s) is look for whatever can most effectively and efficiently boost your business's momentum and lead to increased income.

Naturally, to find your MVP, you assess your franchise and compare it to the rest of the market. As the owner of a Bulldog Subs franchise, you're fortunate. You're able to easily access national and local sales numbers, and compare them to yours.

As it turns out, you sell a lot sandwiches. In total sandwich sales, you're in the 75th percentile nationally, and the second highest selling franchise in your local area. That seems good at first, but then you notice that your total revenue is only in the 50th percentile nationally, and you're only the tenth ranked franchise in your local area. How is this possible?

You pore through the numbers until you find a set that stands out. The national average closing ratio on selling combinations (a.k.a. "combos"), i.e. a sandwich with a side and drink, is 60%. You're closing percentage is only 35%. In addition, you discover that every one of the local franchises generating more revenue than you has a higher closing ratio on combos.

When people go to your Bulldog Subs, as at any other, they have the option of ordering a sandwich a la carte, or else as part of a combo. Individually the two add-ons, side and drink, come at a low cost to you and a significant upcharge to the customer. As part of a combo, you decrease the upcharge slightly enough to make it seem like a good deal for the customer, but there's still an upcharge, and at your franchise you always generate a higher profit margin from the sale of combos than a la carte sandwiches.

You've figured out what's keeping you behind the rest of the pack: combos. They are your MVP, the key to reaching your goal of being the best Bulldog Subs in your region.

Now that you have your goal and MVP identified, it's time to focus on how to use the latter to reach the former. To do this, you're going to need your employees on board, ready and eager to work harder, better, and faster than they ever have before. But they don't care so much about your goal. So you need to give them their own. They need a prize.

3. SHIFT MEETING

On day one of Gamifying your Bulldog Subs, you need to arrange a shift meeting with all of your employees. As you use games, you'll want to arrange shift meetings every day, or else as often as possible in order to make sure your employees stay engaged, understand the games, and know what their targets are. By having routine shift meetings, you'll also have the opportunity to change the games and prizes as needed to keep them fresh (I'll discuss the need for this in more detail later).

At Bulldog Subs, this is your first shift meeting to discuss your games, but treat it like it's the first of many. You want this to be a good experience for your employees, something they look forward to at the start of each day/shift, not dread. If some employees can't make this meeting, you can either have another one with them before their next shift, or you could record this meeting on your cell phone or tablet and have them watch it. Ideally, though, you want everyone possible present for the meeting.

Regardless of how you ensure your employees participate in the shift meeting, it is the essential pivot point you need to start your games, and from then on kick off each daily or new game.

To have an effective shift meeting, you need it to be a pattern interrupt.

Yes, a routine shift meeting is a pattern unto itself, but that's not the pattern you're concerned about here. When your employees get to work, especially on day one of Gamifying your business, they likely aren't mentally at work yet. They could be thinking an argument they had with their spouse, bills they have to pay, an upcoming date, their kid's soccer game that night, or anything else, but you need to break them from their preexisting trains of thought and focus on your MVP(s).

The way you set up your shift meeting is essential to the pattern interrupt. To start, everyone should be required to show up on time. A lot of businesses will put out food, maybe pizza, but while it's okay if you want to put out small snacks, I've found food tends to drag out a meeting and cause people to feel tired (especially high carb and/or fatty foods like pizza). So instead of food, greet your employees with music. The right music affects people almost as powerfully as drugs. It causes the release of endorphins, and can dramatically change or emphasize a person's mood. The key is to find the right music.

Do you know what that is?

It's whatever your employees like. That's all. If they like country, play country. If they like rock, play rock. And if they like hardcore gangster rap, play that. I remember going to watch my beloved Seattle Seahawks play the Green Bay Packers last season. Now I'm willing to bet Pete Carroll, the Seahawks sixty-three year-old coach, probably doesn't listen to the same music as his twenty- and thirty-something year-old players. But when I looked out at the sidelines before the game, the Packers were milling about, going through warm-ups with no obvious enthusiasm, while the Seahawks were bouncing around to music being played by a DJ on their sideline. And coach Carroll was right there getting pumped up with them. Guess who won that game? The Seahawks.

Especially to the millennial generation, music is a major influence on thought and motivation. So now you have music that your employees like playing when they show up for the shift meeting. Make it loud. Force them to raise their voices just to communicate with each other. This will boost their energy. And then, when it's time for you to talk, cut the music off abruptly.

I don't care how many meetings you do this in, when you cut off that music, it will be like you just fired a gun into the ceiling. All eyes will be on you, their own thoughts and patterns erased by the sudden silence.

You were ready to talk to them, but now they are ready to hear you. From this point on, keep things positive and brisk. Don't dwell on any negatives if possible. Tell them your goal, and the MVP(s) you plan on using to reach it, in your case today improving the closing ratio on combos. Theoretically you could dive into explaining the games now, but while these steps are guidelines, remember that you've only told them your goal so far, and no matter how dedicated your employees are, they have their own desires. It's up to you to influence and play off them. To do that, you need a prize.

4. PRIZES

A prize is a lot like a carrot on a string. It's what you use to get your employees to whatever way you need them to go. They do it eagerly because they want that carrot. And even though they eventually can catch that prize, they're will always be a new one for the next game, meaning they can never really catch it.

For even the most exciting, challenging games to truly have an impact, they absolutely must have a prize for the winners.

There are endless possibilities for prizes you can offer. They don't always have to be monetary. In fact, anyone who wins a prize of monetary value will need to pay taxes on it, because it is considered income. So make sure your employees know that up front, and that the prize is accounted for and reported to your payroll department.

That said, over the long-term I've found that **cash is king**.

Many times I've returned to a business, up to years after implementing Gamification, to learn that the games no longer motivate the employees. The truth I've uncovered in every instance has been that the employer stopped paying out cash for one reason or another. Maybe someone else in power vetoed cash, or maybe someone had the idea of switching to gift cards instead of cash. Whatever the reason, as soon as I had them bring back cash, the games increased sales once again.

Cash offers not only instant gratification—many things, even trophies provide that—but it's the physical representation of a win that the highest percentage of your employees will want.

You don't have to break the bank to offer a cash prize. In fact, it's possible (and very likely) you won't have to dip into your own coffers at all when using this system, but for now let's assume the cash prize is a spiff.

A. SPIFFS

A spiff is an immediate bonus or reward for a sale or performance. The key word there is *immediate*.

As human beings, we're wired to seek instant gratification. Sure, delayed gratification can be great, often offering a far bigger, better reward, but waiting is tough, and when we want something, we want it now. This is called "the pleasure principle."

The pleasure principle is the driving force behind the desires I extrapolated earlier from Maslow's hierarchy of human needs. Your desire can be for something as basic as air or as complex as a new car. Whatever it is, you want it, and until you get it, your psychological response will be anxious.

Since cash is the highest percentage prize I've found to appeal to employees, and it's also tangible and should be readily available to you regardless of your business's financial status—how we set up the games will help with this—cash is your base prize to offer.

So back to your meeting at Bulldog Subs. By now you've told your employees that you want to increase the closing percentage on combos. As a prize, you've offered them cash spiffs. For every combo an employee sells, he or she will receive a bonus. Since this is providing instant gratification, you'll need to give them this prize as soon as possible.

This is as basic as a game gets. Call it a spiff or a commission or anything you want. But this isn't really much of a game yet, is it? All you're doing is offering a small bonus.

Don't get me wrong, spiffs work, and your employees will be motivated to sell more combos, but you're trying to create the kind of fun and challenging work environment necessary to reach your goal. To get there, you need employees who are excited to come to work, and committed to pushing themselves to deliver on what you want. To make this happen, you're going to need more than a spiff.

B. THE POT

While you might think that spiffs would be enough to motivate employees, they're not. They just play off their desire for instant gratification. But most likely these spiffs are small, and while they add up over time, they don't have the power of something bigger, a prize like a pot.

If you really want your employees gunning to sell as many combos as possible, you've got to have a pot.

You'll be amazed at how quickly a pot builds up. All you need is a jar, and over time, you fill it with cash (or something else visually appealing to your employees, although cash is king).

Every day your employees will come in, see that pot, and want it. Combine that with a spiff, and now you're getting somewhere.

"Wait," you might be saying. "Spiffs and pots. Why both prizes?"

Because of **Twitch Speed.**

I credit the millennial mentality for spurring on the current Gamification movement. Millennials have grown up with technology intertwined in their lives, and this technology is evolving and growing at an exponential rate.

Remember cell phones ten years ago? Look at them now. The peaks of technology today are increasingly rising at faster and faster rates. Information fuels this growth, and in turn technology creates more and more information. Because of this, information has become one of the most—if the not the most—valuable and prevalent resources we have today. And so we as a species are evolving to keep up with it.

Having lived their whole lives amid this boom of information, millennials are the generation most adapted to it. The inundation of information has caused their brains to become used to fast-paced processing, and to function at "twitch speed."

Technology isn't going anywhere. That means neither is twitch speed. And this means it's the responsibility of all generations (not just millennials) to adapt and embrace these realities in order to stay relevant.

Your employees have a need for speed, whether they're aware of it or not, and it's your job to feed into it.

Up to 70% of companies trying to implement major changes fail, not because their ideas were bad, but because they couldn't get their employees on board. This is why you need more than a spiff and more than one prize. And your game itself is going to require multiple games.

That's how you keep up with twitch speed. By deploying different types of games and prizes, and continually changing things up, you'll create fresh, dynamic challenges, keep your employees engaged, and your momentum going.

So you're going to have to get more creative by incorporating more challenges and bigger prizes into your system. "Wait," you say again, "bigger prizes? My Bulldog Subs franchise already isn't meeting my goals, how am I going to afford this?"

C. PRIZE FUNDING

If you have a product or work in sales, the answer is simple: pack it into the dead cost of the items you want to sell. I usually pack $2 for anything that sells for under $50, $5 for $50-100, $10 into the cost of anything that sells for $100 - $250, $20 for items between $250 and $500. Adjust up or down as you see fit, but that's just a starting point. You can always adjust it later. For your combos, if they're selling at $7 each, raise the price to $7.50, putting the extra charge directly toward the prizes.

If the cost of the prize money is packed into the cost of the item, the customer is paying for it, and your personnel expenses don't increase. It's that easy.

If you're not selling a product or generating direct revenue onto which you can tax the cost of the game, you can offer prizes of non-monetary value, at least initially, until you've built up your game coffers enough to cover the prizes as a cost of doing business.

So you've started with a spiff. This gives your employees instant gratification. That's one prize. For every combination they sell, they get $0.25. This leaves you with $0.25 leftover from every combo to put toward the pot.

For every combo sold, the pot gets a contribution of $0.25. You can set the pot contribution at the same amount as the spiffs or differently, but we're keeping things simple here and making the pot the same. Only one person or team will win the pot when the game is over, whether that's at the end of the week, month, quarter, or whenever.

Now we're getting somewhere. The spiffs provide your employees with instant gratification in small amounts, while the pot offers the allure of a big, potentially life changing prize. Believe me, these pots can add up quickly, and even a pot as small as $100 can have a huge impact on your employees' morale and performance.

So maybe that seems like enough for now. But picture the faces of the employees around you. We're in a meeting after all. What do they see?

I'll tell you: They see their boss making them promises with empty hands.

D. SHOW AND TELL

Remember the iPhone my friend offered his sales team at the Hemp Fest? When his sales people saw the phone, their eyes lit up with desire. We were showing them what they wanted. That's what hooked them.

When running a game, the more you **show** the prizes, the better performance will be. And the bigger the prize you show, the more the players will want it.

With spiffs your employees will be instantly gratified. But for the pot, use a jar or jug of some kind that lets them see the money, and put it somewhere out of sight of any customers.

As the pot fills, make sure to keep it safe, but also to show it to them every time you put money in. More than that, make it clear that the money you're putting in has come directly from the upcharge on the combos.

The $0.50 upcharge is designated as their prize money from the start. They only get a portion of it as a spiff, but the whole thing is still theirs. This is the key to making them truly want that pot.

Even if the money isn't coming directly from their sales, perhaps because they aren't selling a product, as long as you make it clear that the money is theirs to lose, this will still be effective.

Let them see and feel how their contributions pile up. As far as each of your employees is concerned, the money in the pot comes directly from them. This sense of contribution has a powerful impact. It imbues a sense of ownership over the pot, and they'll want to do whatever it takes to ensure that no other player or team wins *their* pot.

That's when you've really got them.

But that also takes a bit of time to make happen. What about right now, when you're standing in front of them with empty hands. The money for the pot hasn't been made yet. You need one more prize, one to show them up front.

This needs to be something worthwhile, that everyone wants, and the bigger, more exclusive and more desirable, the better. Like that iPhone. It was sold out everywhere, so everyone wanted it. You need a grand prize.

E. GRAND PRIZE

When implementing a new system or a larger goal than current performance can justify, it's possible you'll encounter some resistance from employees. I find that a grand prize often best helps to immediately change the minds of the team and to get them at least trying, which starts momentum.

But if this is something you're offering up front, then even if you draw its cost against projected income from the game, it's going to cost you money, right?

It's possible, yes, but at the same time the grand prize doesn't have to be expensive or cost anything at all. It just has to be something everyone wants.

Often a premier parking place in front of the building or closer to the office for a month yields better results than a Hawaiian vacation. This works because every time the winner parks right out front they get a subtle reminder that they're a winner. This ego boost makes them feel good. They won't want to lose the spot. And this desire drives continued performance.

If you can't offer premier parking or would prefer something else, perhaps a service your company provides could make for a great grand prize. Too often employees don't spend the time or money to use the very things they sell. I've seen this work with spas giving away a Pamper Package as a grand prize or flower shops offering weekly fresh flowers for a month delivered to anyone an employee chooses. It's something they wouldn't normally treat themselves to, and it promotes the company in a fun way.

Of course, you could splurge on a prize. If you do, there's nothing wrong with that either. My friend splurged on those expensive iPhones for the Hemp Fest, after all. But if you do buy a grand prize, say a brand new TV to offer your employees, make sure you have it with you to show them from the start of the game.

Regardless of what you choose for your grand prize, all three types of prizes I've described—spiff, pot and grand—are the basis of making Gamification work. The prizes are what stack the deck full of incentives for your employees to buy into the game, and then keep buying in.

5. SCHOOLYARD

Now let's get back to your meeting. You've told your employees that there will be spiffs and a pot from the sales, and since your Bulldog Subs franchise happens to be in a busy strip mall, you've taken the whole team out front and showed them two parking spots that you've reserved for the winners to have for a month.

"But what's the game?" one of them asks. "How do we win?"

To set this up, we're going to make your workplace a schoolyard, i.e. we're going to create teams.

Research has shown that when a player is performing for the benefit of a team, they will increase performance by as much a 30%, depending on the game or task.[9]

We've also learned that strategic play increases when players are grouped up, just like on the schoolyard when we were kids. Groups communicate and help each other through a team culture. Even in the most competitive dog-eat-dog sales environments, teams work. Unlike that car sales person who couldn't care less how his peers perform, he is now encouraged to help and root for the others on his team.

You could create a game that pits each employee against each other, and if you have fewer than four employees you'll likely have to do this. But when possible, I run team games 80% of the time, and sometimes more often, because they simply work the best.

As individuals, players carry all the weight, but only for themselves. When an individual falls behind, they could lose motivation or begin to feel like they've already lost. Alone, they're more apt to give up.

Being on a team nips this negative outcome in the bud. A team diffuses responsibility while simultaneously creating a greater sense of responsibility. As part of a team, an individual must carry his own weight, while also being aware of his teammates' contributions. They motivate and push each other. Even though failure is still a possibility, it's a lot easier to get yourself up off the ground when someone else offers you a hand.

I've also found that small teams work best. They increase productivity and enthusiasm, and while nobody feels like they're getting lost in the group, the team prevents them from feeling too pressured to perform.

When you have your team working together and helping each other toward a shared goal, you also get the side benefits of them sharing and training each other.

Teams share in victory and defeat, as well as most challenges along the way. These shared benchmarks lead to a greater sense of responsibility, because while it's one thing to play for yourself, when others are depending on you, you have to deliver for them too. This selfless responsibility leads to higher productivity through coordination of efforts, maximization on individual skillsets, and using the team to mask weaknesses.

Finally, teams foster better competition by creating the perception of more beatable antagonists. Feeling like it's *me against everyone else* can seem daunting or even impossible to some players, but on a team the mentality becomes us vs. them, and victory is more attainable.

America is a country itself rooted in this mentality, beginning with the small upstart colonies who once took on an unbeatable British empire.

You don't have to like sports at all to recognize that we embody this mentality today through our nationwide love affair with team sports. You almost definitely wouldn't be able to beat LeBron James in a game of basketball one on one, but as part of the right team, even you might stand a chance of claiming victory against him, or at least have more hope of doing so.

The advantage of teams isn't just based on hypotheticals. Statistically a team gives a player a better chance to win. If you have four players, as individuals each would only have a 25% chance, but as part of two teams they each have a 50% chance. And when a player wins, they get a boost in morale. That benefits you. And even if that player wasn't the top dog this time, just being on the winning side will push him going forward, and he will likely strive to become a top dog. So now through teams you're reaping the benefit of more individually driven, better employees too!

* * *

We're back in the shift meeting now. You've got your employees gathered, you've told them about your goals, the MVP, the prizes, and now you've told them that they'll be forming teams for these games.

To ensure fairness, each team will include one cashier and one sandwich maker. You'll attempt to pair teams together on shifts, but your employees' schedules vary, so when teams can't be paired together on a shift, the unteamed sandwich maker and cashier will split the spiffs and points from their sales (I'll explain *points* shortly).

This might seem counterintuitive to having teams, but you have to work with the business you have, and splitting things up this way will keep each day interesting and full of competition.

You can form the teams however you want. You could take the top performers from the previous day or week or month and assign a weaker performer to each of them. You could go by the current shift schedule. Or you could let them choose their teammates themselves.

Once the teams are formed, the rules of the game need to be laid out.

6. THE GAME

You'll want to clearly explain and write down a list of the rules.

Games can and will evolve, but it's important to be as clear as possible about the rules at all times.

For this game, the fundamentals seem simple. Each team will receive a spiff of $0.25 for every combo sold, while contributing $0.25 to the pot. When non-teammates are paired together, they'll split the spiffs and contributions to the pot as well. This is seems easy enough, right?

Here's where things get more interesting.

There's still a pot and a grand prize. And being the best performing team is not going to guarantee winning at least one of these prizes.

"Wait," you say, "the best team won't get at least one of the big prizes?"

That's correct.

If all prizes were only given out based on direct performance, inevitably one team would eventually rise above the rest, whether at an early stage in the game or late, and the other team or teams, realizing they face certain defeat, would lose steam. No matter how strong the team bond and mentality, facing a loss is facing a loss. And the last thing you want is for there to be a period in your game when any of the teams slow down.

You stacked the deck to get them invested in the game. Now you have to stack it to keep them in it. To do this, you need to even the odds. You're going to need games within the game.

7. GAMES WITHIN THE GAME

When stacking a deck, the more cards you move, the more control you have over the outcome. We've created multiple prizes to instill and satisfy different desires in your players, as well as meet their needs for instant and delayed gratification. This motivates them to get started. By using different types of games in your overall game, you'll keep them motivated.

So let's go back to the shift meeting once more. At this point, your Bulldog Subs employees *know* that you want them to sell more combos. They've been formed into teams, and for every combo a player sells they get a spiff from part of the upcharge, and the rest goes into a pot. There is also a grand prize of two premier parking spots for one month. That's all clear. What they *don't know* yet is how they can win the pot or the grand prize.

The possibilities for how you implement other games are endless. When you reach the upcoming "Games" section of this book, you're going to find colorful pictures and breakdowns of games that I've personally tested and witnessed succeed.

To keep things simple, we're going to stick with specific examples, but keep in mind that these examples are potentially interchangeable, and with each iteration of the game you will certainly want to change things up.

To set up the new games, you explain that while the spiffs will stay the same and keep going into their pockets, you're going to use a point system to help them reach the other prizes. You don't have to use a point system, and there may be instances when you won't, but I've found it's the best way to keep track of the teams' progress.

"So we're going to win those other prizes based on who gets the most points?" one of the employees asks.

"Not quite," you say.

"Then how?" another employee says, chin-lifted, eyes-wide.

You've got their attention and you know it.

"Those prizes are will be awarded to the winners of games within the game. But to play those different games, you're going to have to use the points you earn from your team's sales."

You'll likely have to explain things a bit further for them here, and you will be able to do that once you've finished this book, but what I most want you to grasp right now is how the games all tie together. It doesn't matter if the primary game involves selling a product, collecting information, or doing anything else. The players or teams earn points for their progress, and they get to use those points to play the other games, through which they can win at least one or more of the prizes.

A. THREE TYPES OF GAMES

For the games within the gam, there are three different types you can choose from: Games of Chance; Games of Skill; Games of Knowledge

Different players have different mindsets. No matter the environment, not everyone is going to enjoy the same things or have the same abilities. That's just part of being human. And that's why having different types of games is so important. Each type of game has a different appeal, but between the three, you'll be able reach just about anyone, and give everyone a fair chance at winning one of the prizes, often even late in the game.

So which games are you going to use in your Bulldog Subs?

You could use a game of chance.

B. GAMES OF CHANCE

Roll the dice, draw a card, spin the wheel. Whatever you do, provided you play by the rules, these are games where you can't control the outcome, or at most have limited control.

If you like games of chance, you're probably a gambler at heart. That doesn't mean you gamble, but I'm willing to bet you'd like it. I'm a bit of a gambler myself.

Roulette is a game of chance, because you as a player can't practice or use any strategy to change the roll of the ball or the number it lands on. The dealer can, but as a player you cannot.

I've found that Games of Chance appeal most to risk takers. These people are often dopamine driven, maybe high ceiling low floor sellers. They enjoy the thrill of uncertainty, of the rush almost as much as they want to win. Chances are they've had multiple jobs. They're willing to go on a limb, a hunch, take a chance.

At the same time, games of chance are also best at keeping the field level. Perhaps the game you choose to set up is a lottery. Every five points earns a team a ticket. Sure, the more tickets a team earns the better chance they have of winning, but all it takes is one ticket to win. And even an underperforming team will be compelled to keep trying to earn more tickets right up till the very end of the game.

Games of chance represent one end of the game spectrum. There, all players start with a theoretically equal playing field.

The other two types of games I'm about to explain fall at the opposite the end of the spectrum. These are games of skill and games of knowledge.

C. GAMES OF SKILL

Shoot a ball, throw a dart, perform a routine. A game of skill is one that tests the body, requiring existing physical abilities in its players. The mind plays a big role here too, but in unison with the body (unlike games of knowledge). The more skill a player has, as a direct product of practice and talent, the greater that player's odds of winning will be.

If you turn on your TV at any given moment I guarantee you can find a game of skill. There are so many channels devoted to these games, i.e. sports, because we admire skilled performers. To many of us, games of skill represent the peak of human physical capability.

For these games, I've found that they appeal most to people who like to control their own destiny. Even if they aren't the hardest workers in your office, these are people who are very motivated when they're interested in something. And if you can hook their interest in your game, you can harness what could be immense latent potential within them.

D. GAMES OF KNOWLEDGE

Like games of skill, games of knowledge are also subject to the players' ability, except games of skill test the body and mind, while games of knowledge purely test the mind.

The best example of a game of knowledge I know of is a crossword puzzle. Your ability to solve a crossword puzzle does not depend on your physical state. It depends entirely on your knowledge, experience, and intelligence. You know an answer because you studied about it, it's something you remember from your life, or it's a result of your deductive reasoning.

This type of game appeals to analytical and intelligent people, but also to those who might not have the physical capability to succeed at games of skill, or the risk-taking mentality to embrace games of chance.

In a game of knowledge, all a player has to do is use his mind. Even if a player believes he isn't as smart as another, he has the potential to focus on what he learns, and prepare himself for the game.

It's true that both games of skill and knowledge aren't going to be balanced from the start. Pre-existing abilities will have a major impact, and superior players are likely to rise to the top. While this can be motivating to inferior players, who then practice or study so that they can better their chances of winning, you can set up more balance through how you set up the teams, and by determining which skill or knowledge games to use. After you use one game that a particular team or player succeeds at, you should switch to a new one that a different team might be better at.

Of course, some games are going to overlap. Many chance-based games can be won through skill or knowledge over luck. Likewise games of skill can be won by luck or knowledge, and games of knowledge won by luck of the draw.

It's up to you which games you choose for your real business.

At your Bulldog Subs, the spiff has already been established as earned directly through sales, but you still have two more prizes for the teams to win, the pot and the grand prize.

8. CHOOSING YOUR GAMES

Although many games overlap categories, let's say that you can only choose two out of the three games, since you only have two prizes remaining.

Right away this tells me that one of the prizes should be won through a game of chance. This ensures that all of the players start out with an equal chance to win at least one of the bigger prizes. That doesn't mean you can't combine a game of chance with another category, but there needs to be a primary element of chance.

So which of the prizes should be won by chance? In real life, this is going to depend on your situation. You're going to assess the two remaining prizes. In your Bulldog Subs, one is a pot of money that comes from upcharges on combo sales. The other is two parking spots awarded to a team. Which one of these, if won by luck, would be better?

Neither.

Gamification is a system, and you're going to be using it indefinitely. If this time the pot is won by luck, next time it can be won by skill. The same goes for the grand prize. All that matters is that players' or teams' chances to win any prize is woven directly into their pursuit of your goal.

All you have to do now is make a choice.

So let's just say that this pot will be won by a game of skill, darts, and the parking spots by a game of chance, a lottery.

9. SET THE RULES

Once you've chosen your games, it's your responsibility to make sure the rules are as clear as possible, and that all players know them. Before your shift meeting, take the time to think out the rules. Try to anticipate any potential issues. Then type them up and print them out as a reference for the players.

For the pot, you've decided to go with darts as a game of skill because it's fun, reasonably cheap, and small enough to fit into the backroom of your Bulldog Subs. You then tell the players that for every five combos they sell, their team gets one turn at the dartboard.

Obviously there are many games you can play on a dartboard. And you can explore as many of them as you want as you create new games. Since this is the first time you've ever used any games in your Bulldog Subs, you decide to make things as basic as possible. The first team to land five bull's-eyes wins the pot.

The more you think about it, the more the game becomes clear. Every ten combos earns a team one turn of two throws. Each player can throw once, or choose to let the other player take both throws. If a player isn't present, the other player can choose to take both throws, or hold one or both of them off until the other player is present.

To make things a bit more interesting, you decide to give every team the freedom to choose to accumulate turns so that they can take several turns in succession if they choose.

You'll keep track of each team's number of turns on a dry erase board next to the dartboard, with the numbers all backed up privately as a failsafe.

To make sure business keeps going uninterrupted, you'll have throwing times set aside for 11am, 2pm, 4pm, and 8pm.

If a team hits five bull's-eyes and the pot is won before the end of the overall game, then a new pot is created, and a new game of darts begins. If a pot hasn't been won by the end of the game, it's added into the next game's pot, and the game of darts continues.

Of course, you don't want to hand a series of paragraphs like these over to your players. So once you've flushed out the game rules, write them down as clearly as possible. Below is an example:

Bull's-eyes For Cash

Objective:
The first team to hit five bull's-eyes wins the pot.

Game Rules:
1. *For every 10 MVPs, a player/team earns a turn (2 dart throws).*

2. *A team may decide which player throws.*

3. *A player may throw for an absent player without permission.*

4. *A player may choose to wait for an absent player to return before throwing.*

5. *Teams may accumulate turns and take multiple turns at one time.*

6. *Turns can only be taken at times designated by the game leader.*

7. *If a team hits five bull's-eyes, that team wins the pot.*

8. *If a pot is won before the end of the primary game, a new pot is created.*

9. *If a pot is not won before the end of the primary game, the pot carries over to the new primary game.*

10. *If a pot carries over, so too do all teams' scores.*

This kind of list is much easier for players to understand. The language is a tad pedantic, but that's okay. You want to be as clear as possible to avoid any possible misinterpretation of the rules.

Anyways, now that we've set up your dart game, let's move on to the parking spot lottery.

You've already decided that for your Bulldog Subs this premier parking grand prize will be won through a game of chance, a lottery.

A lottery, or raffle, is basically to a pot, except the winner is determined purely through a draw, making luck a major element.

Through my own experiences, I've found that lotteries, either on their own or as a part of yet another game, are an extremely effective way to incorporate sales, distribution, or whatever you're having your employees do with your MVPs into a game of chance. Because a lottery relies on a final draw, it allows you to set a specific end date for this game, while also giving every team a chance to win right up until the moment someone's number gets called.

The simplest way to set up this lottery is give each team a ticket for meeting a certain benchmark. For your Bulldog Subs, I can think of a couple different options. You could reward gross sales. For every ten combos sold, in addition to a turn a darts, each team gets a new ticket added into the lottery.

Or you could reward efficiency. At the end of every day, you could go through each team's numbers and award a ticket to any team that closed better than the 60% national average. For doing better than 75% they get two. And above 90%, they get three. For 100%, you tell them you'll throw in a hug. Just kidding.

Of these two options right now, I prefer the second one: efficiency.

Although the second option creates more work for you, in calculating those numbers for the game, you're actually doing yourself a favor. As you use gamification in your business, you're going to track your progress and statistics anyway. You need to make sure it works, don't you? By making these percentages essential to the function of the game, this one a lottery, you effectively force yourself to track the numbers.

So here's how you would break down the lottery for your employees:

Parking Lotto

Objective: *Have your number drawn to win your team two premier parking spots in front of Bulldog Subs for one month.*

Game Rules:
1. *For every day ended with better than a 60% closing ratio on MVPs, a player earns his team one lottery ticket.*
2. *Higher than 75% earns that player's team two tickets.*
3. *Higher than 90% earns that player's team three tickets.*
4. *Teams can win as many tickets as possible.*
5. *The winning lottery ticket will be drawn by the game leader on the last day of the month.*
6. *The team with the winning numbers will get to keep the two premier parking spaces for thirty days.*
7. *If the winning lottery ticket is not claimed immediately, the winning ticket holder will have three days to claim it.*
8. *If the winning ticket is not claimed after three days, a new winning ticket will be drawn, and step 7 repeated.*
9. *If the primary game ends before the lottery has ended, the lottery will continue until a winner is chosen.*

There you have it. Your games are almost set up. I have a just a few more things to address first.

In reading these examples, you might have noticed the phrases "For every 10 MVPs, a player earns," "game leader" and "primary game."

I use the phrase "For every X (number) MVPs, a player/team earns" and specifically avoid using the word "sold" or any reference to sales, because this book is aimed at all businesses, and I don't want to cut out any potential business owners or managers who aren't using games with traditional products. As I've said before, MVPs can be just about anything you deem as a means for reaching your goal. In your own, real rules, you can obviously phrase this part however you want.

As for "game leader," that just refers to you, the boss.

And now this brings me to the last important element of your games.

10. START THE CLOCK

As with any game, it's your responsibility to ensure there is ticking clock, i.e. an ending. For some games a point total you or the game rules sets will dictate the end, like your dart game above. Other games will dictate their own end, as a crossword puzzle does. While other games, such as a lottery, require you, as game leader, to set a date for when to determine a winner and end the game.

There is an exception. In our written rules example, "primary game" refers to the overall game outside these games, pushing MVPs for spiffs. While players win in these scenarios, it can be hard to decide when to end these games, and when to keep them going.

Unlike my friend who had his sales people collect business cards at Hemp Fest, which was a specific length, giving him a timeframe, in this instance, the primary game has no clear ending. Theoretically, they could keep pushing combos for spiffs forever. So you need to decide on an end point.

You could decide to end the game every time the pot is won, or the grand prize, or you could simply set a time period for the game to last. It's up to you how you end it; all that matters is you create a timeframe for the game, so that you can evaluate your results and implement any necessary changes, e.g. trying out a different price point on your MVP, raising or lowering employee payouts, changing the MVP, adding a new MVP, etc.

* * *

Now, at last, your deck has been stacked. It really didn't take all that much to do it either, did it? Just the same ten steps you see below:

Ten Steps To Stacking The Deck

1. Establish Your Goal

2. Choose Your MVP

3. Shift Meeting

4. Prizes
> *a. Spiffs*
> *b. The Pot*
> *c. Prize Funding*
> *d. Show and Tell*
> *e. Grand Prize*

5. Schoolyard

6. The Game

7. Games Within the Game
> *a. Three Types of Games*
> *b. Games of Chance*
> *c. Games of Skill*
> *d. Games of Knowledge*

8. Choosing Your Games

9. Set the Rules

10. Start the Clock

As you move forward with games at your Bulldog Subs, you don't always have to use at least one game of chance. I suggested that here because this was the first time you'd Gamified your franchise, and for the initial effort, I find it helps to guarantee your players that at least one game starts out all of them on equal ground.

In addition, you don't have to use two additional games like we did here. You could just use one, or you could you could use more than two, or combine multiple games. For example, you could combine your lottery with a game of knowledge. Instead of earning tickets through MVPs, the teams earn questions, and if they answer the questions correctly, then they win tickets. Like I said before, the possibilities for games are endless.

Of course this has all just been an example. In real life, I won't be there when you set up your games. You'll have this book to help you create and choose games, and following the upcoming games chapter, you'll find a chapter in which I address and offer solutions to some of the issues that you might encounter in Gamifying your business, although ultimately these are *your* games, and you need to make sure you think them through carefully, trying to foresee any issues that might arise, while being as clear as possible about the rules, and always aiming to keep things fresh.

If you follow the system I've outlined in this chapter, as you did with your hypothetical Bulldog Subs, you will Gamify your business. And almost immediately after sending your employees out to start playing—yes, I said *playing*, not *working*—you will see positive results.

THE GAMES

Examples Of Games You Can Start Using In Your Business Tomorrow

BASKETBALL

Supplies Needed:
Dy Erase Board
Dice
Shoebox Lid

Preparation:
Draw a basketball
court in the bottom of
a shoebox lid. Use the
court to roll your dice.
Pick Teams.

Game Rules:

1. Seller earns a dice roll with each unit sold.
2. Seller rolls dice in the court.
3. Keep track of each sellers point totals on the board.
4. For every MVP, a player earns a "shot," or dice roll. Mark the points scored by each roll on the board.

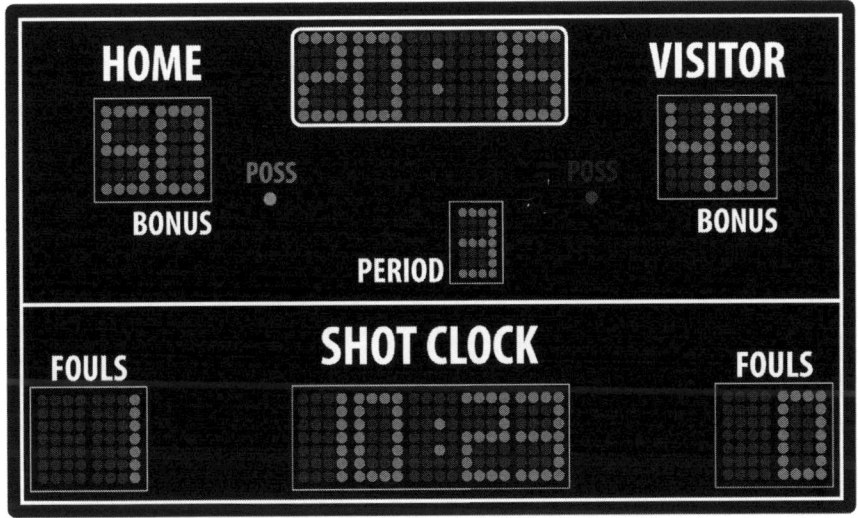

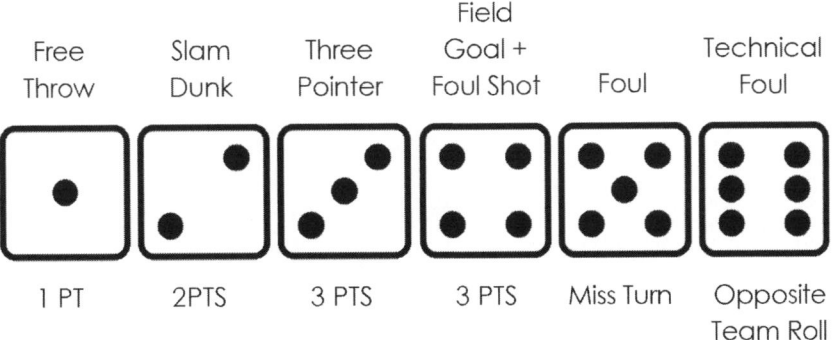

BATTLESHIP

Objective:
Sink your opponents ships to win the game.

Preparation:

Make or print two blank Battleship
grids for each team.

	A	B	C	D	E	F	G	H	I	L
1										
2										
3										
4			X							
5						X	X			
6		X						X		X
7				X						X
8	X	X						X		
9										
10										

Type of ship = Size
Aircraft Carrier = 5 | Battleship = 4
Destroyer = 3 | Submarine = 3
Patrol Boat = 2

Game Rules:

The game is played on four square grids, two for each team. The individual squares on the grid are identified by letters and numbers on the vertical and horizontal axes. On one grid, the team arranges ships & records the shots by the opponent. On the other grid, the team records their own shots. Before play begins, each team arranges their ships secretly on the grid, either horizontally or vertically without overlapping. The type of the ship determines the number of squares each ship occupies on the grid. After the ships have been positioned, the game proceeds in a series of rounds. In each round, a player earns a turn via an MVP. The player announces a target square on the opponent's grid. One target can be selected for every MVP. If the opponent's ship occupies one of the target squares, then it takes a hit. When all of the squares of a ship have been hit, the ship is sunk. If at the end of a round all of one team's ships have sunk, the game ends, and the other team wins.

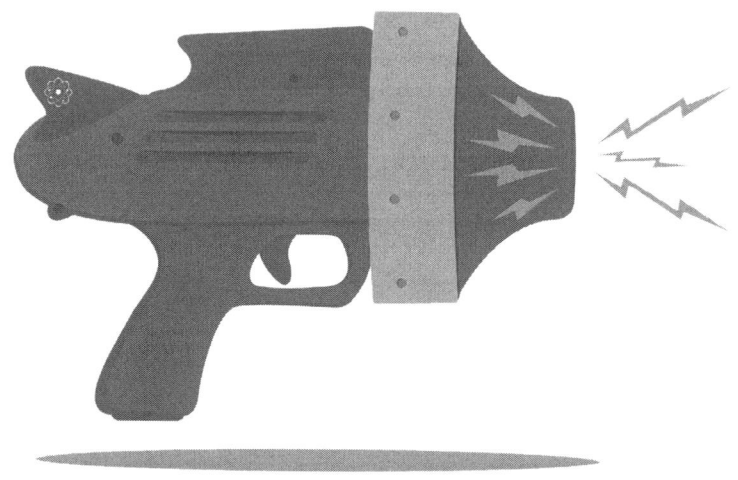

BONUS BLASTER

Objective:
Complete the most events by utilizing
(selling, gaining, distribution, etc.) the most MVPs

Supplies Needed:
Game chart
Marker

Game Rules:

Each MVP earns a player a bonus. Once all services have been sold, the player is eligible for bonus level payouts. The team with the most services sold wins the accumulated pot.

1. Print off one chart for each team.
2. Pick teams.
3. Each service sold pays the amount shown in the box, as well as a set amount to the pot (dollar amounts and services are for example only).
4. Each player must complete his EVENT to qualify for the INDIVIDUAL BONUS LEVEL.
5. Every MVP sold after completing the event pays as shown in the bonus box.
6. The team with the most services sold wins the pot.

Brake Flush $5	Injection Service or Induction $5	Nitro or Coolant Flush $5	Alignment $7
Brake Flush $5	Injection Service or Induction $5	Nitro or Coolant Flush $5	Alignment $7
Brake Flush $5	Injection Service or Induction $5	Nitro or Coolant Flush $5	Alignment $7
Brake Flush $5	Injection Service or Induction $5	Nitro or Coolant Flush $5	Alignment $7
Brake Flush $5	Injection Service or Induction $5	Nitro or Coolant Flush $5	Alignment $7
Brake Flush $20	**Injection $20**	**Coolant $20 or Nitro $10**	**Alignment $20**

BOUNCER

Objective:
Bounce a predetermined number balls (10 or 15 is a good amount) into the cups before the opponent (the higher the target number, the harder the game becomes).

Supplies Needed:
25 Cups
Water
Marker
Ping Pong Balls

Preparation:
Fill each cup halfway with water and arrange the cups into a triangle (simliar to a rack in pool). If you don't have different colored ping pong balls, label each ball for each team.

Game Rules:
Each player gets one shot per MVP. A player must bounce the ping pong ball into a cup. If a ball is made into a cup, that team owns the cup. If a player from the opposing team makes a ball into an owned cup, they take over the cup (cup is always owned by the last person to shoot into it).

How to win?
1. Be the first to own the number of cups decided at the beginning of the game.
2. Be the team with the most owned cups at the end of the game (as determined by the game leader).

BUST THE BOARD

Objective:
Pop balloons to win the bonus inside. The team with the most points at the end of the game wins.

Supplies Needed:
Foam
Paper
Balloons
Darts or toy gun
Cardboard box

Preparation:

1. Make a game backboard on which to hang balloons (here are some options: use a Paper Easel Board, a Cardboard Box, or Foam. You could also use build a longer-term backboard with wood).
2. Insert pieces of paper with bonuses written on them inside the balloons, and then fill them with air.
3. Use a toy gun or dart to "bust" the balloons.

Game Rules:

1. A player gets one throw for every MVP.
2. A player is awarded the bonus inside any balloon that they pop, while the team is awarded a point.
3. The team with the most points at the end of the game wins the pot.

- CADDY STACKS -

Objective:
Using a flat surface, stack 3 golf balls upright as many times as possible within 1 minute.

Supplies Needed:
A stopwatch, 3 to 9 Golf Balls,

Preparation:
Divide sellers into teams.

Game Rules:
1. Each MVP gives the player 1 minute to complete the objective as many times as possible.

2. Each time the player does complete the objective, he earn points toward the team.

3. If manager is limited on time, make the player sell more units for a chance to play.

4. Use a stopwatch to time players, and mark how many times they complete the objective.

CARD NINJA

Objective:
Earn the most points by throwing cards at an object.

Supplies Needed:
Watermelon and a new set of poker cards.

Preparation:
Place the object 6 feet away from the strike zone.

Game Rules:
Each MVP earns a player/team three cards. The player then throws the cards at the watermelon in an attempt to get a card stuck. Each time this is done successfully, the team is awarded a point. The team with the most points wins the game."

CONNECT THE DOTS

Objective:
Connect dots to form boxes for your team. The team with most marked boxes wins the game.

Supplies Needed:
Dry erase board or printout of the dot grid.
Two separate color markers.

Preparation:
Draw or print out the dot grid. Divide into teams and assign team names.

Rules:
For every MVP, a player earns a turn. The dots must be adjacent, but can be anywhere on the page. The goal is to close four sides of a box. Each time a player creates a box, he gets a point and another turn. Be sure to mark all boxes with the team's initials. It is legal to use the opponent's lines to close or build a box. The team with the most points at your predetermined end of the game wins!

CHUTES & LADDERS

Objective:
Be the first team to reach the finish line.

Supplies Needed:
Dry Erase Board
Markers (3 colors)
Post It notes
Pick teams

Preparation:
Draw a replica Chutes and Latters game on the dry erase board (or use the game board if you have one). Assign a symbol or color to each team and label post-it notes accordingly. You will use the post-it notes as your game pieces.

Game Rules:
For every MVP, a player earns a dice roll. According to the roll, advance the team's game piece. If the player lands on a ladder, they move up to the corresponding space, while a chute drops them down. The player or team that reaches the finish line first wins the pot.

36 35 34 33 32 31
25 26 27 28 29 30
24 23 22 21 20 19
13 14 15 16 17 18
12 11 10 9 8 7
1 2 3 4 5 6

CONNECT FOUR

Objective:
Be the first team to connect four of
your team's color in a row.

Supplies Needed:
Connect Four game set
Two Teams

Game Rules:
For each MVP, a player gets to drop a red or
yellow game piece into the grid. Once a team con-
nects four, that team either earns a point or wins the
game. In the event of a tie, the game starts over and
continues until one team wins.

CUBILETE

Objective:

The team/player with the most points at the end of the game wins the pot.

Supplies Needed:

Poker dice

Dry erase board or easel

Writing utensils for board

Preparation:

Create two teams and choose captains.

Write the winning hands on the dry erase board.

Game Rules:

Aces are wild, and can be played as anything.

For each MVP, a player earns a series of three dice rolls using all five dice. After each roll, the player can remove any dice he wishes to keep and re-roll the remaining dice. After all three rolls, the player either collects points according to the grid, or busts with zero points.

Scoring:

Five Aces =10 points

Five Kings with no wild Aces = 5 points

Five Kings including wild Aces = 2 points

Five Queens including wild Aces = 1 point

Five Jacks including wild Aces = 1 point

Five Tens including wild Aces = 1 point

Five Nines including wild Aces = 1 point

CUTTHROAT

Game Rules:

Cutthroat is a game of speed and endurance. For each MVP, a player earns a chance to roll the dice and move across the board. Players can take turns moving the team marker and collecting points along the way. Once a player crosses the finish line, his points are locked in and can't be taken away. If the opponent passes him before he crosses the finish line, the opponent takes all of his points, hence the name, "Cutthroat." Once across the finish line, a player adds his points to his team's total, and then starts over on the board. *The team with the most points at the end of the game wins. Team with most points after a determined amount of laps (set by the game leader) wins.*

Objective:

Score points for your team as you move along the board.

Preparation:

Draw a figure 8 graph like the one below. Write in each box whatever you like, or follow designed game board below. Pick two teams and assign two captains.

DEAD WEIGHT

Objective:

Collect the most points by the time the grid is filled. And don't get "fired!"

Supplies Needed:

Dry Erase Board

Different colored markers

Game Rules:

For every MVP, a player earns a turn to pick a square and fill it in with the team's color. The goal is to collect three squares in a row. Once a team has three squares in a row, draw a line across them to connect them together. A player cannot borrow a square from a square that is already a part of a point. This is a game of strategy, as the teams try to block each other from scoring points. The team with the most points once the grid is entirely filled in, wins! The following morning, each team must fire a teammate, releasing their "DEAD WEIGHT." Voting is done confidentially through a secret ballot. After the ballots have been cast, the "DEAD WEIGHT" will switch teams.

Objective:

Race along the track as you sell units to complete laps for your team.

Supplies Needed:
Dry Erase Board
Post-it Notes

Preparation:
Draw a racetrack on the dry erase board and section it off into the number of MVP sales or gains you want to accomplish for the day or allotted time period of the game. Draw two or more race cars on post-it notes to represent the teams. Pick teams.

Game Rules:
1. For each MVP, a player gets to advance his team one space.
2. The team with the most laps in a timeframe determined by the game leader wins.

DECEPTION

Game Rules:
In a clock-wise rotation, start with whomever is holding the 2 of spades. He shouts out the number of 2s being placed face down on the table. (Remember, this can either be deception or the truth). After the player has placed cards on the table, opposing players can either call out deception/liar/or bullsh*t to contest the cards being played. If the player playing the card is correctly placing down what they stated, the player calling out "deception" takes all the cards in the center. If the player calling out "deception" is correct, then the person playing the card picks up the center pile. If no one calls anything, the next player goes. After each (5-10 min) round, count up each player's cards. The total is added to the teams score. The total is added to the team's score. The objective is to collect no points each round with no card or the fewest possible cards left. The score is calculated just like golf. The lower the score, the better.

Objective:
Call your opponents' bluffs to make them pick up cards – the player with fewer or no cards at the end of the round wins the game.

Supplies Needed:
Standard deck of cards.

Preparation:
Shuffle the deck of cards very well. Then choose 3 or more team captains. Have timed intervals, and make everyone aware of the times to play. (e.g. - 9am, 11am, 1:30pm, 3:30pm, etc.) Play one quick 2 min. round in the initial meeting so that everyone understands the game.

DICE

BASEBALL

OBJECTIVE:
Score the most points for your team
by earning dice rolls with sales.

Supplies Needed:
Dice
Scoreboard (I'd suggest a whiteboard to
make the score as visible as possible to all players)

Preparation:
Assign a value to each of the possible number
outcomes of the dice roll, 2 – 12.
For example:
2 is a home run (all baserunners score).
6 or 8 is a Single.
5 or 10 can is a Double.
3 or 11 is a Triple.

7 is an out, and the player's turn is over.
9 is a Double Play, loss of turn, and loss of next
team turn.
12 is a Triple Play, loss of turn, and next two team
turns.
Draw a baseball field out on the whiteboard.
Divide into two even teams if possible.

Game Rules:
For each MVP, a player gets a series of dice rolls to
score points, until he is "out." Have both teams in
attendance, and take turns back and forth. The
team with the most runs scored (points) wins the
game. A run is scored by forcing a "player" across
home plate. Each team gets three outs per inning. If
a player gets more outs on a roll than the team has
remaining in the inning, the extra outs are ignored.
There can be as many innings as needed, but if
possible you should decide before the game starts.

DICE-O-RAMA BOWLING

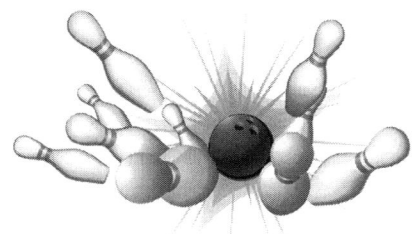

Objective:
Be the player with the best score at the end of the game by knocking down "pins" with dice rolls.

Supplies Needed:
Dice

Game Rules:
Each player is awarded a chance to bowl per MVPs.
A player rolls the dice twice with each turn.
If a player rolls a pair of sixes (12) on his first roll, it is a gutter-ball - No Points. If he rolls a five and a six (11), it is a 7/10 Split. Roll a pair of fives (10), that's a strike! All other rolls represent face value. For the second roll, only use one die to get remaining "pins."

DICE OF LUCK

Game Rules:

After each team has decided on a number they must try to roll it. Points are earned according to the following or any variation of:

1st roll = 10 Points
2nd roll = 8 Points
3rd roll = 6 Points
4th roll = 4 Points
No more rolls after 4. If Team A picks to lock in number 8 as their number they have 4 tries to try & get an 8 with the two dice. If they land an 8 on the 1st roll, they are awarded 10 points. If they land it on the 5th roll, they would be awarded 2 points.

Objective:

Collect more points than your opponent by rolling your number with the fewest rolls. A player earns a chance to roll through MVPs.

Supplies Needed:

Dice

ELECTRONIC ROULETTE

Objective:

Score the most points for your team using MVPs as a way to earn chips and ultimately earn points for your team.

Supplies Needed:
A computer or tablet with the roulette game downloaded plus a dry erase board.

Preparation:
Put the game up on your computer or tablet.
Select two team captains to choose teams.
Create a grid that motivates whatever you are wanting to sell more of. E.g. If you want to sell more alignments, give Alignments = 50 chip value that the player can choose to bet with. Coolant, brake, P/S, = 25 chip value, and Nitrogen service = 15 chip value.

Game Rules:
A player gets to play one round per MVP. A player can choose to bank 10 points earned to the team total (no more no less than 10 per roll). The player then wagers the rest of his/her earnings to try to score more points toward the team. The end of the game is predetermined by you, the game leader.

Ex. If you want to sell more alignments, give Alignments = 50 chip value, that the player can choose to bet with.

FILL OR BUST!

Objective:

Outscore your opponents

Supplies needed:

A Fill or Bust game set

Game Rules:

For each MVP, a player earns a turn. The player starts by drawing a card. This sets the player's goal. The player then rolls the dice, unless they've drawn a "no dice" card, also known as busting (bust = no score, turn over). After the first roll, the player can choose to stop rolling and keep his points, or he can set aside his scoring dice and continue rolling. If the player chooses to continue rolling, he runs the risk of losing all of his points, if none of the dice score on the next roll. If the player gets a "fill," i.e. a scorable point, he can earn bonus points from the draw cards. The player also has a chance to continue rolling by first grabbing another card, and re-rolling all six dice. In order to score bonus points, you must draw 1 of 54 cards with a positive bonus, not negative. If a player draws a 300 bonus point card, he must roll a "fill" before busting in order to collect the bonus.

How To Score: 1s and 5s are what to mainly focus on, along with triples. Below is the breakdown for points

5s = 50 Pts	1s = 100 Pts
3 x 1s = 1,000 Pts	3 x 2s = 200 Pts
3 x 3s = 300 Pts	3 x 4s = 400 Pts
3x 5s = 500 Pts	6s = 600 Pts

A straight, 1-2-3-4-5-6, is the best possible dice roll at 1,500 points.

FLASH SCRABBLE

Objective:
Outscore opponents by scoring the most points.

Supplies Needed:
The Flash Scrabble game set
Backup batteries (just in case)

Game Rules:
For every MVP, a team can play one round of Flash Scrabble. The game device automatically adds up all words spelled, and will advise a player at the end of his turn. The points from all correctly spelled words are then added to the team's total. In addition, a team can choose to wager additional turns in one round. For example: if a team has earned eight turns, i.e. eight unplayed games, but wants to divide it into only two games, they can do so by having the player annouce the number of turns wagered before the start of the round. In this case, if the player wagers 4 turns and scores 10 words, that player's team would be awarded 40 points.

FOR-GET-IT

Game Rules:
A player receives a turn for every MVP. The player then rolls the dice to try to get a pair or more of one number. After each roll, the player can choose to collect points and end his turn, or continue to roll for more points with the remaining dice. If three of the dice form the words "For-Get-It," the player loses his turn and all points gained

Scoring:
A pair adds up the total of the dice. So two 3s would yield 6 points. If you roll more than a pair, your score is multiplied.

4 of a kind = 2x
5 of a kind = 3x
6 of a kind = 4x

Objective:
Outscore your opponent using the For-Get-It game set.

Supplies Needed:
Dry Erase Board + Marker
For-Get-It game set

Preparation:
Assign captains
Pick teams
Create a scoring grid

GO
THE
DISTANCE

Objective:
Score points for your team by making shots.
The team with most points at the end wins.

Supplies Needed:
Measuring Tape, Ping Pong Balls, Stopwatch,
and Shot Glasses or red solo cups.

Game Rules:
For each MVP, a player gets one minute to try to get
as many balls in the cups as possible by rolling them
down the measuring tape. The amount of points
assigned to each cup is predetermined by the game
leader. You can base this on distance or difficulty.
Points are earned by making balls into the designated
shot glasses or cups. Once the minute has ended,
points are tallied up and added to the team's total
points. The team with the most points by the end of
the predetermined time period wins the game.
Note: Players receive a "Foul" if they touch the
measuring tape at any time. They may only touch the
housing of the measuring tape itself. If a player
gets 3 fouls in a round, they lose their turn, and
no points are given.

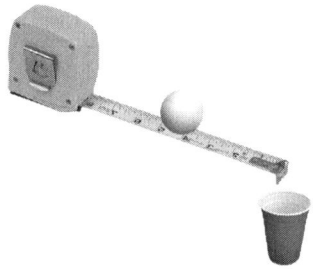

GUMBALLERS

Objective:
Win rewards from the gumball machine based
on the color selected.

Supplies Needed:
Gumball machine with gumballs.
Quarters or coins for machine (if required)

Game Rules:
For every MVP, a player earns a turn to twist the knob.
Create a gumball reward chart similar to the one below
(dollar amounts are for example only)

GREEN – DOUBLE
PINK - $12
BLUE - $10
PURPLE - $8
ORANGE - $6
YELLOW - $5
WHITE - $3

HANG 'EM HIGH

Game Rules:
For every MVP, a player earns a turn to add a body part to the other team's gallows. The player may also choose to remove a body part from his own team's gallows, however, he must pay a fee to the pot in order to do so. As game leader, you determine the number of rounds or when the game ends. The team with the least amount of hangings wins.

Objective:
Don't get hanged!

Supplies Needed:
Dry erase board
Dry erase markers

Preparation:
Draw a hangman gallows on the board for each team.

- HIGH -
LOW

Objective:

Have the highest value card in hand.

Supplies Needed:

Deck of playing cards

Game Rules:

For every MVP, a player plays a game of High Low against you, the dealer. The player draws a card first, and then the dealer. High card wins. You can run this game as a one-off or create teams and your own tournament structure.

HUMPTY DUMPTY NERF

Objective:
Shoot bricks out from under Humpty Dumpty
to knock him down and win the pot.

Supplies Needed:
Dry Erase Board and a Nerf gun with
extra bullets.

Preparation:

Draw out a brick wall, 12 bricks tall by 12 bricks wide. Draw a Humpty Dumpty or a head of your choice on top of the wall. If the darts do not stick to your surface, use a colored marker to color the tips of the darts, so they leave a mark indicating your team. Choose 2 team captains.

Game Rules:

For each MVP, a player gets to shoot at the wall for points (number of shots is at your discretion). A player collects 1 point for each brick shot or "hit." A player can double his points by shooting any of the 1st row of bricks at the top, but if he hits Humpty Dumpty, his team is penalized 20 points. After each brick is hit, mark an X on it. This brick cannot be shot again. When all of the bricks under Humpty Dumpty have been hit, the game is over, and the team with the most points wins the pot.

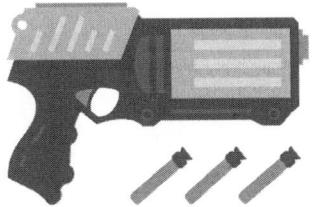

JACKS BACK

Objective:
Collect as many jacks as possible to earn points or bonus money.

Supplies Needed:
One standard Jacks game set

Game Rules:
For every MVP, a player bounces the ball and picks up as many Jacks as he can before the ball bounces again. This game can be played individually or as a team. The jacks can represent real dollar amounts or points. You predetermine the end of the game as a point/dollar total or timeframe.

– JENGA – BOOM

Objective:

Pull and place as many blocks as possible in the allotted timeframe determined. The team with the most points wins the pot.

Supplies Needed:

Jenga Boom game set

Marker

Preparation:

similar to Jenga Greed

Game Rules:

For each MVP, a player gets to play one round of the game. The player then has roughly 30-45 seconds to pull and place as many blocks as possible. After the tower is leveled by the bomb, the round ends. Add up the total points & award them to the player's team. The game ends at a specific time or point total predetermined by you, the game leader.

JENGA GREED

Objective:
Pull blocks to win points for your team. Most points wins the game.

Supplies Needed:
A Jenga game set and a marker.

Preparation:
Use the marker to write a point total from 5-30 (in increments of 5, 10, 15, 20, etc.) on each block. Build the Jenga tower as designed. Divide the employees into teams.

Game Rules:
For every MVP, a player gets to pull one block. Add the points written on each block pulled to his team's total. If the tower is knocked over by the player, his team receives a 50 point penalty (-50 Points from score).

JENGA TOWERS

Objective:
Build a tower larger than your opponent.

Supplies Needed:
Jenga game set (two for larger stores) and
a ruler or measuring tape. Stopwatch & Dice (Optional)

Preparation:
Divide employees into teams.

Game Rules:
For every MVP, a player gets one block. Once a team
has enough blocks, they can start to build their tower.
The team with the tallest tower wins the game.

Optional Game Rules:
If the store sell enough MVPs, use dice to
determine the number of blocks each player gets.
You can also use a stopwatch, and have head to head
battles, once both teams have enough blocks.

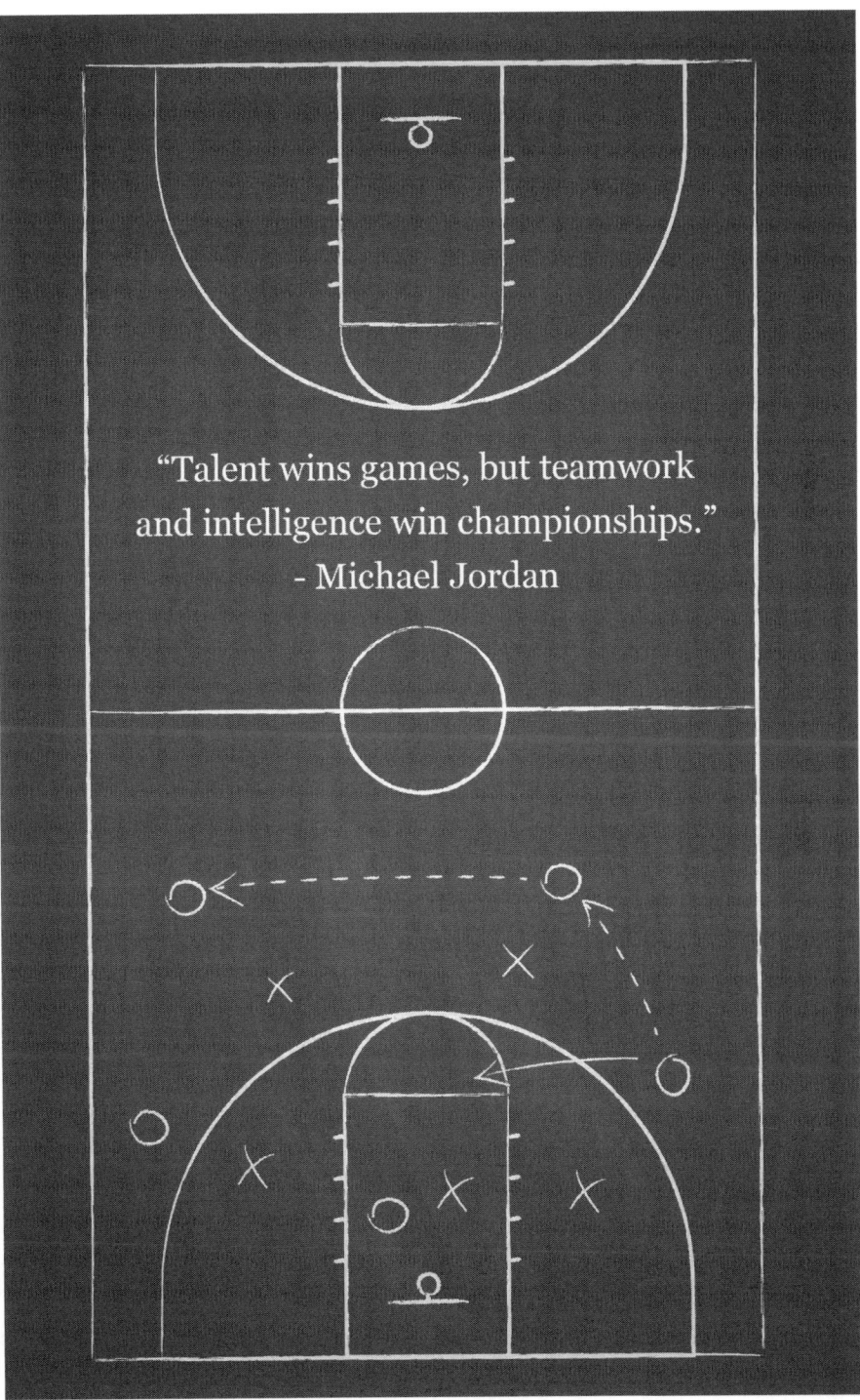

"Talent wins games, but teamwork and intelligence win championships."
- Michael Jordan

LIVE BASKETBALL

Objective:
The team with the most points wins.

Supplies Needed:
A small fun-size kids basketball rim,
or a full size basketball board and basketball.
Colored Tape

Preparation:
Set up rim/hoop in a safe location where players
can shoot. Use tape to mark 3 ranges of shooting.

Range 1 = 2 points
Range 2 = 5 points
Range 3 = 10 points
(Range and points can be adjusted accordingly)

Game Rules:
A player earns 3 shots per MVP. Each time a
player shoots and scores, his points are added to
his team total. If a player makes all 3 shots in a
row, he gets a bonus shot to collect more points
toward the team total. The end of the game is
predetermined by the game leader.

Objective:
The team that scores the most points by throwing footballs through a suspended tire wins the pot.

Supplies Needed:
One standard size tire.
A few Footballs
One tire holder/ a location where the tire can be elevated about 4ft. off the floor.
Tape/Floor markers

Preparation:
Preparation is easy if the tire holder is already built, or if you have a good location for it. If you don't, you'll have to set it up yourself. Make sure it's sturdy. Then use the tape or markers to mark off three different distances for throwing. Choose team captains.

Game Rules:
For every MVP, a player earns three throws. A player-can choose to throw from the 1st marker for 1 point, the 2nd marker for 5 points, or the 3rd marker for 10 points. The team that has the most points at the end of the game, or that reaches a predetermined total first, wins the pot.

BONUS: If any player makes three throws in a row in one turn, he earns double points.

Objective:
Advance further than your opponent on
the game board to win.

Supplies Needed:
One Logos board game box, or the app on your Apple or
Android phone (the physcial game is more interactive).

Preparation:
Set up game board and cards.
Divide the store into teams.
Choose team captains.

Game Rules:

For each MVP, a player gets to roll a die to determine the color space he moves his game piece to. Once the player has moved, the game leader picks a random card from the pile and reads the question to the player. If the player answers the question correctly, he stays where he landed and re-rolls the dice. If the player answers incorrectly, he returns to his previous position. A player continues to play off of one MVP until he fails to answer correctly.

MINESWEEPER

Objective:

Flag the most mines while navigating through the minefield better than your opponent.

Preparation:

Print one blank grid for each team, and then use the example below to make a minefield key.

Game Rules:

For every MVP, a player earns a turn to pick a square. Check the key and reveal the number in the chosen square. The number revealed tells the player how many mines are located in connecting squares. The object is to find and "flag" the most mine squares correctly without landing on them.

MYSTERY ENVELOPE

Objective:
Earn the spot as top seller to win the game.

Supplies Needed:
Three identical envelopes

Preparation:
Place a different amount of money in each envelope. Ex. $20, $50, or $100. Make sure the money is wrapped in white paper as to not show through, and make sure the envelopes are weighted the same.

Game Rules:
The top MVP seller earns the Mystery Envelope pick. Give your top seller an opportunity to change envelopes.

NERF DARTS

Objective:
Shoot the target to earn points
for your team.

Supplies Needed:
A couple of Nerf guns
A target
High energy

Preparation:
Set target up in a secure location.
Practice a couple of shots for
maintenance approval. Divide
employees into teams.

Game Rules:
Players get X amount of shots per
MVP. You determine X. Add up total
numbers of hits, and apply it to the
team total. Predetermine the
lengh of the game either by point
total or timeframe.

OH CRAPS!

Objective:
Earn as many points as possible. The team with the most points at the end of the game wins the pot.

Supplies Needed:
One set of dice
Backup set of dice

Preparation:
Divide store into teams.

Game Rules:
Each player gets 3 dice rolls for every MVP. To earn points, a player rolls two dice and tallies the total number of pips (dots) showing. After each roll, the player can choose to collect his points and end his turn, or continue rolling. A player gets a maximum of three rolls to collect as many points as possible per MVP. Any time a 7 or 11 is rolled, the player loses all points earned in that series, and his turn is over. A player's total points are added to his team's score. Game duration is determined by the game leader.

OVER UNDER

Game Rules:

Note: You may play the game following the instructions, but I always get better results by just playing with the game cards and dice, but no Game Board.

Below are my rules:
For each MVP, a player has the opportunity to roll the colored die that comes with the game set. The game leader then grabs the same color card that the die landed on.
If the player gets the answer correct, he or she is awarded 1 point, and rolls again. An incorrect answer ends the turn. MAX of three rolls per turn.

Objective:
Score the most points.

Supplies Needed:
Over Under board game set.

Preparation:
Divide the players into two or more even teams and you're ready to start. A good way I've found to boost morale for this game is to pick a few of your favorite cards out of the bunch to read out loud during your shift meeting, so they understand the concept, and can see how fun they are.

POP-UP PIRATE

Objective:
Score the most points using the
Pop-Up Pirate board game.

Supplies Needed:
Pop-Up Pirate game set

Preparation:
Set up Pop-Up Pirate (following the instructions)
Divide the sword colors by teams.
Choose 2 to 4 teams (depending on size of store).

Game Rules:
Each player gets to insert one sword into the barrel per
MVP. Whenever the Pirate pops up, that player's team is
awarded 1 point. Then reset and start again. If there is a
tie, go into sudden death. Take turns, with each player
from each team inserting a sword one at a time until the
pirate pops up. That team wins.

-QUALIFY-

Objective:
Total 25 points or more by rolling five dice over a series of five rolls. Add up the pips (dots) on the dice to score.

Supplies Needed:
Five Regulation Dice

Preparation:
Have your 5 dice ready.
Choose 2 team captains to pick teams.

Game Rules:
Having earned a turn through an MVP, a player declare how much he is willing to wager (in MVP units). Let's say he wants to wager 3 units. The player then takes 5 dice and begins the first of 5 rolls. After each roll, the player can set aside any high scoring dice and continue to re-roll the remaining dice. After the player's final roll, add up all pips face-up on the dice. If the total is 25 points or more, the player (or team) wins their wagered amount. If the dice add up to less than 25, the player collects no points. Number of rounds or duration of game determined by game leader. Winner gets the pot.

– RING TOSS–

Objective:
Toss rings or horseshoes at a distant target,
earning points for each one that lands on the target.

Supplies Needed:
Ring toss set or horseshoe game set
Bottles or stakes

Preparation:
Create two teams and a starting line.

Game Rules:

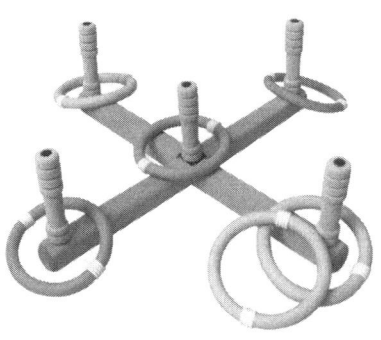

For each MVP, a player gets
to toss "X" amount of rings
at the target (for larger
stores make "X" a smaller
amount). Bonus rings are
awarded to any player that
sells multiple units in the
same R.O.

SALES OLYMPICS

Objective:
Sell units and earn the most medals for your team.

Game Rules:
The Sales Olympics are designed to motivate your team to sell specific products. Each team is made up of 5 Olympians. There are 6 events in the Sales Olympics.

One Olympian from each team must compete in 2 events. Whichever Olympian completes his event the fastest wins the gold medal for that event. For each event, a player must sell three predermined MVPs, as well as a "Wild Card" product of the player's choosing. The team with the most gold medals wins the pot!

You may help out a fellow Olympian by donating one of your MVP sales to their event, but it will cost your team a predetermined (by the game leader) amount that goes into the pot.

Preparation:
Draw or print the Sales Olympics game board as seen below. Pick teams.

Supplies Needed:
Paper or dry erase board marker.

Product 1	Product 2	WILD	Product 3	JAVELIN

Product 4	WILD	Product 5	Product 1	50 YARD DASH

Product 1	Product 4	Product 3	WILD	LONG JUMP

WILD	Product 4	Product 1	Product 2	SHOT PUT

Product 6	Product 4	WILD	Product 7	HURDLES

Product 6	Product 8	Product 1	HIGH JUMP

WILD	WILD	WILD	WILD	WILD	RELAY

SHUT THE BOX

Objective:
Have the lowest score

Supplies Needed:
Shut the Box game set

Game Rules:

For each MVP, a player gets a turn. The player has two dice. If numbers greater than 6 remain on the board, the player must roll both dice. Otherwise the player can choose to roll one. A player can use the total number he rolls to close numbers in the box. So if he rolls a total of 9, he can eliminate the 9, or else a 5 and a 4, 6 and 3, etc.

If the player's total does not match any numbers or combinations of numbers in the box, then his turn is over. If a player closes all numbers out, he has "Shut the Box" and automatically wins the round. If the player doesn't shut the box before his turn ends, the game leader then plays his turn. If he gets a lower score than the player, the player's points are added to his team's total. If the leader does NOT get a lower score than the player, the leader's total is subtracted from the team's total. Number of rounds or duration is determined by the game leader.

SQUARE SHOOTER

Objective:
Create the best poker hand with three or fewer rolls.

Supplies needed:
Square Shooters game

Preparation:
Divide the store into two teams.

Game Rules:
Players earn a set of three dice rolls per MVP. After each roll, the player can choose to keep any number of dice & re-roll the rest.

If a player ends up with 1 pair, their team gets 1 point
flush = 5 pts
5 of a kind = 10 pts

THE MILLION DOLLAR GAME

MORE MVPS = MORE CHANCES TO WIN THE POT.

Supplies Needed:
Scratch tickets
Raffle tickets (optional)
Jar (for tickets)

Preparation:
Divide employees into teams (if you choose to).

Game Rules:
1. For each MVP, a player gets to play a game
   that gives him a 50/50 chance to win a scratch ticket
2. The 50/50 game should be one of the player's
   choosing. Give him a list of options (flip a coin,
   draw a high card, hand of blackjack, etc.)
3. If the player beats you, give him a scratcher and let
   him scratch it. If he loses, give him the scratcher and
   let him scratch it as well. The difference is that if he
   beats you, let's say at blackjack, he gets to keep any
   winnings on the scratcher. If he loses to you, any
   winnings from the scratchers go into the pot.
4. The team with the highest point total
   (determined by MVPs), wins the pot.

Alternate Ending:
Instead of awarding the pot to the team with the most
MVPs, you give it away through a raffle. Give each a
player a raffle ticket for every MVP he sells. At a
predetermined time, you then draw the winning ticket
from the jar and that team takes the whole pot.

TUMBLIN' MONKEYS

Objective:
Drop the fewest monkeys.

Supplies Needed:
Tumblin' Monkeys game set.

Preparation
Set up the Monkeys' tree. Insert the colored sticks into the open holes in the tree. After inserting all of the sticks, drop the monkeys over the top opening (game is now ready). Choose team captains, and have them pick teams.

Game Rules
For each MVP, a player gets to roll the die. They then remove a stick of the same color rolled from the tree. If a monkey falls, the player must keep it.

Once all the monkeys have fallen, the player with the fewest monkeys wins.

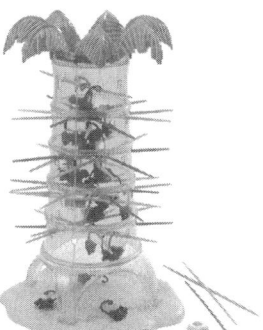

ULTIMATE MASTERMIND

Objective:

Decode the game leader's code to win.

Supplies Needed:

Ultimate Mastermind game set

Preparation:

You'll want to read the instructions for a better understanding of this game, but to set it up, first get your mastermind code in place. Then choose two team captains to pick teams. Have the teams each take turns trying to decrypt your master code during the shift meeting so that they'll have a good understanding of the game.

Game Rules:

Have the teams each take turns, earned via MVPs, trying to decrypt your master code. The team that figures it out first, wins.

Objective:
Score the fewest points to win

Supplies Needed:
One or more decks of UNO cards

Preparation:
Choose team leaders and select teams.

Game Rules:
Deal a hand of cards to one representative for each team at the start of the day or during the pre-shift meeting. For each MVP, the player earns a turn to play an UNO card. Follow the intructions for the game itself (I'd suggest reading them through and making sure all players do). When a player has one card left, he calls out Uno. When he plays that card, the turn is over and all other teams must add the sum of their remaining cards to their score. When a team reaches 500 points or another predetermined score, the game is over, and the remaining team with the lowest score wins.

WILD CARD
POKER

Objective:
The team that wins the most rounds
(or redermined total) wins the pot.

Supplies Needed:
2-4 decks of poker cards (the more the better)
A poker card holder (optional)

Preparation:

Shuffle all poker decks together. Selects captains to choose teams. Determine three to four daily time intervals to have the players come in, and play their best poker hands, e.g. 10am, 1pm, 4pm, and leave the final round for the end of the day. Also decide what the wild card(s) will be at every timed interval. (e.g. at 9am, aces are wild (or just one ace), at 1pm, wild cards are 7s, etc.) Give one representative from each team 5 cards to start the day .

Game Rules:

Each player gets one poker card per MVP. The team then adds the cards to the starting five they received at the start of the day/shift. Until the round is played, the team continues to build its best possible five-card hand. The player/team with the best hand wins the round. Continue playing until each team has exhausted all of their five card hands. Cards cannot be played twice. Once all hands have been played, deal five new cards to each team representative, and have the teams start working toward the next round. The game ending is predetermined by the game leader, either at a point total or in a specific round (should be at the end of the day).

THE HOUSE

"Play long enough, you never change the stakes. The house takes you.
Unless, when that perfect hand comes along, you bet and you bet big, then
you take the house."
-Danny Ocean, *Ocean's Eleven*

By now you've read all about how to Gamify your business. You know the steps to take, you've learned how to play the games, and maybe even started setting up your own system. I hope you're excited and optimistic that this is going to work and you will reach your goals.

At the same time, Gamification is new to you, and I'm guessing there might be a little voice in your head that tends to raise questions about something new. You're banking a lot on these games, potentially increasing your customers' cost or investing your own funds. Yes, these games stack your deck, but do they really give you the perfect hand? Do you they really make you Danny Ocean?

Let's imagine you have that perfect hand.

You're playing poker. The cards are smooth against your fingertips. You look at them for a second time just to make sure they're exactly what you thought they were: two red aces.

Then you shift your glance up, making sure that you've really got this hand won.

Your heart thumps in your chest as you train your focus on the three cards lying face up in front of the dealer. Countless colored lights, flashing signs, and faces blur into the background. As do the mess of chips gathered in the center of the table and the many different sounds swirling around you. Oxygen rich air fills your lungs, and the slight scent of a fellow player's cigarette drifts up your nose. There they are: two black aces and a random four of clubs on the flop.

There is not a better hand you could have right now. You've flopped "The Nuts." All you have to do is play it smart, and find a way to entice the other players in the hand to bet as much money as possible so that you can get your payday.

You look to the six other faces that encircle the table. Expressions vary from stoic and sunglasses-masked, to nervous, or calmly focused. Three other players remain in this hand. You want their money. And you're going to get it.

It's your turn first. You know from playing at home, online, and watching way too many episodes of the World Series of Poker that the worst thing that can happen now is for you make a bet that causes those other players all to fold, so you decide to check.

But then the next player bets. It's a medium-sized bet designed to say "I've got an ace. If you don't believe me, you can pay to see it."

You know this because you've been playing at this table with this player long enough to know a little about him. He's good. He plays the odds, and when he bluffs, he does it from a position of strength.

The other two players fold.

Without flinching, you look over at the remaining player. Cool confidence stares right back at you.

You briefly debate internally whether to raise or call him. Heart beating faster, you're excited, but part of you wonders what he might have. You raised before the flop and he called, indicating that he probably has two high cards or else a pocket pair. You're not sure. You only have two certainties: he can't have an ace; and he has a lot of chips in front of him.

Since he's appeared to be good player so far, you assume that if you raise he'll realize you have at least one ace. Unless he has two fours, giving him a full house, which is highly improbable, the only way he'll call you is if he either somehow doesn't believe you or is on a flush draw, with two clubs in his hand, and hoping for another to come on the turn.

Then again, you want to get the most money possible out of him. And your best chance of doing that is for him to make a hand that he believes is better than yours. If he's on a flush draw, you want him to make it. And you want him to think you have an ace when he does.

So you raise. Yes, if he's bluffing he'll fold. If he has another pocket pair, he'll probably fold. He could even fold if he has the flush draw. But by raising you're telling him that you want him to fold, and that also tells him that you only have one ace hidden. If he calls and gets the flush, he's going to think he has you beaten.

You hold your breath for a second. Slow exhale. He debates. *Come on*, you think, *call me*.

Finally he says, "Call."

The dealer burns a card, snaps off the turn, and the five of clubs appears. Bingo! If he was drawing on a flush, he just made it.

You feign a slight sigh, nothing too noticeable, but enough of a reaction that if he spots it he'll think you're disappointed in seeing another club.

Then you lead out with a medium-sized bet. It's purely to show defeat. If you just check, and he bets and you raise that bet, he might realize you have the nuts. But by betting a medium amount, you're telling him that you have an ace and are afraid of those three clubs. Either he has the flush and he'll raise to push you out, or he'll fold.

He raises. Now you've got him.

When you push all your money into the pot, he looks confused. *Why would you do that?* he appears to think. But he can't bring himself to fold his flush, so he calls.

You smile as you turn your cards over. You don't even look at the river card because all you can see are those chips in front of him, all those chips that are about to be yours.

Or so you thought...

Next thing you know the dealer is taking *your* money. What the heck? You check the river. It's a three of clubs. Hold on a second...

He has the six and seven of clubs. You were right, he had the flush, but also a straight flush draw. And he hit it. You had the perfect hand and he beat you.

It had seemed impossible for you to lose. Everything was in your favor. At the beginning of the hand *you were Danny Ocean*. By the end of it, that other guy was. And as you watch the dealer take your money, all you can do is put more in or go home a loser.

This is what happens to a card player.

A card player is someone who goes into entrepreneurship, a business, or a management position trying to win. They see the game and their goal is come out on top of it. What they win could be a pot, a trophy, or even a massive return on an investment or their business.

Danny Ocean is card player.

You are not Danny Ocean. And you are not a card player.

If you watch closely, you'll notice that with every round of betting, the dealer takes a couple chips for the house. This is the rake.

No matter what happens, the dealer rakes the house's share, and the house gets paid.

Sure, in a casino luck factors into all games the house plays, but luck is not a factor the house gives a damn about. The house doesn't wait for the perfect hand. The house doesn't care which player wins. The house is built to survive. It takes in earnings with steady, strong momentum, based on statistics that are always in its favor. That's not luck. That's stacking the deck so that no matter what happens, the house always wins.

By Gamifying your business, you become the house.

As the house, you'll want to ensure that your house is build to stand over the long-term. I've already explained how you need to vary your prizes and games in order to keep up with twitch speed and maintain players' interest and engagement, but other issues might arise that could affect the effectiveness of your games.

When a casino takes a big hit by a Danny Ocean-type player, that's a problem. But think about what happens when a player wins big. Does the pit boss start panicking? Do the games shut down? Of course not.

The casino's system has been designed to account for players like Danny Ocean. Before the big winner has a chance to count his chips, I guarantee that one of the floor bosses will be at the table, offering him tickets to a show, or a room upgrade, or a free dinner. Whatever the offer is, it's meant to keep him around and encourage him to gamble more, because regardless of how much he's won, the longer he plays the more the odds move toward the house's favor that he'll lose the money he won back.

You have your goals, you know how to set up your games and prizes, and you know why they will work. Now all you have left to do is to make sure that the odds are always in your favor, so that when the games build your momentum, you never lose it. To do this, you need to be ready for any Danny Oceans (i.e. potential issues) that show up.

* * *

I've always enjoyed gambling. Maybe that's why I was so drawn to Gamification. Even though this is a system that shifts the odds immensely, it still allows me to play games, gamble, and have fun while helping businesses achieve success.

I could write down a dozen different reasons for why I like gambling, and they're all valid; however, ultimately I like it because gambling venues themselves have been specifically designed for me to like them. Their decks are stacked to hook me, and Danny Ocean, and you.

In creating this system, I've drawn research from history, independent studies, and first hand experiences to show you how and why games have such a powerful impact in businesses. Now, to ensure the long-term sustainability of Gamification, I'm taking my cue from the best game sustainer I know: casinos.

My friends and I used to do a "guys" trip every year to Las Vegas for the annual motocross race.

Like I said, I've always enjoyed gambling, but in my early twenties, when we first started taking this yearly trip, my experience was mostly limited to friendly bets and scratch tickets. When it came to games like blackjack, roulette, and craps, I'd messed around with them a bit, but was definitely a beginner.

Then one year my friend Marco and I ended up getting stuck having to wait for the rest of the group while at the MGM Casino. Marco suggested we play blackjack to kill some time.

I liked gambling, so even though I didn't know the game that well, I was down to play.

We found a table with two empty seats and sat down. I won a few hands, lost some others, and made sure to get a free cocktail, but nothing wild happened at first.

Then about thirty minutes later, two of the other players suddenly got upset. They had both just lost a lot of money and one of them said, "It's not the cards, and it's not the dealer, but this is bullshit."

They both stared daggers at me as they cashed out and left.

I was confused. What had I done? I hadn't taken a dime of their money.

After they left, I naively asked the dealer what happened. He said that I had hit on a twelve when the dealer was showing fourteen. "That's technically not the right move by the book," he said.

I had played bad fundamental blackjack, at least according to this "book." If I had stayed, which was the statistically correct play, the face card I got would've gone to the dealer instead. He would've busted and those other two players would've won. So as far as they were concerned, it was my fault they'd lost.

"Don't worry," the dealer grinned, "it's your game. Play it your way."

At the time I shrugged it off. I could do what I wanted with my money. But in hindsight, what he said was truer than anything according to "the book." Sure, if I had it to do now, I would've been a team player and not hit, but if playing by the book was a strategy that worked, casinos would be losing enterprises. And the house always has the edge. People aren't robots. They have their own desires, and they play for them. That's what the house counts on, just as you need to in your business.

Since that day, I've returned to Vegas many times, and gambled a lot, both winning and losing. Through it all, I've always been fascinated with how the house gets and maintains its edge.

Depending on the game, the house edge is as low as 1% (blackjack), or as high as 20% (slots). As a player, you might research ways to beat those odds. Casinos want that (provided you stay within the rules). They need you to think you can win. That's what keeps you playing.

You think you can win because of dopamine. Dopamine is the brain's pleasure chemical, and the same one your brain releases when under the influence of love or drugs. The rush of a win gives you a *high*. The casinos want you to feel that. It's a feeling that supersedes reason or logic. And like drugs or even love, once you feel it, you'll do anything to feel it again, and the more you feel it, the more you need it.

That's how they hook you. Winning five dollars gives you that good feeling your first time at the table, but by the second time five dollars doesn't do anything. You want to win ten. And the next time you want twenty.

It's the casino's goal to keep you chasing that feeling, to need that fix. That's why the vast majority of people who try gambling once inevitably try again. Gambling is a one hundred billion dollar industry that all but two states have tapped into, because people are wired to do it.

A casino game is like a beautiful but crazy lover. You know she is bad for you, but you can't help wanting her. And the casino does everything in its power to make you look past rationality and keep wanting her.

Remember that free drink I got earlier? It's part of making you stay. Everything is. From the lighting and music, to the labyrinthine layouts, and even the smells, casinos are designed to keep you inside and playing games that are stacked against you.

All the while, they give you just enough of a chance to win to trick your brain into thinking that the next big payout could be around the corner. When your eyes see two cherries instead of three on a slot machine, you should know that you lost and the next turn will be a wholly independent variable, but your brain can't help thinking, "So close, keep going!" In fact, your brain can't even tell the difference between an almost-win and an actual win. As the wheels slow on that second cherry, your brain surges with dopamine. That's what heightens the addictiveness of it; you lost, but got dopamine anyway. So your unconscious brain takes it as a win and wants more.

That's a big reason why the house always wins. Because they make you think you're winning even when you lose.

In your business, you don't have to go anywhere near the lengths that casinos go to. You don't have the time or money, and this book plus basic market research will be more than enough to suffice for you.

But I want you to keep the casino in mind as you set up your system.

The more carefully you build your games, and the more attention you pay to the details of what works and why, the better results you will see. And like a casino, your success depends on your players' involvement, so while from day one, every member of each team might be gung ho and ready to go, some might not be, or something might happen during a game, and you need to be ready and able to deal with any kind of problem, whether it's a Danny Ocean, or just a beginner who might be losing interest because of sour grapes.

***

Problems come in all shapes and sizes, but over the years, however, I've found that the majority of problems tend to fit into one of five categories: Haters, Hesitators, Cheaters, Losers, and The Hangover.

In this section, I'm going to address each of these types of problem, and how to deal with them.

1. HATERS

Let's go back to Bulldog Subs and pretend you're in the backroom once more, explaining the games your employees are going to play to help increase the closing ratio on combos, your MVP.

You've told them all about the prizes, split them up into teams, and given your best pump-up speech.

Most of the players appear to be excited. Working at Bulldog Subs is a low-paying, entry level job that offers little in the way of fun, but you just gave all of them a chance to make more money and actually enjoy what they're doing.

Then you notice one of the players rolling his eyes. His nose wrinkles and he lets out an audible sigh. You can hear the words he's about to say before they even come out of his mouth.

"This is stupid," he says. Or else maybe "My team sucks."

Having walked into a room or business cold and implemented Gamification hundreds of times, I can pass along my experience dealing with the players who don't want to join in on the fun right away, or at all.

I call them TOs.

TO is short for Terrell Owens. Maybe you've heard of him. He was an incredibly talented wide receiver in the NFL, and while on the San Francisco 49ers he made one of the toughest catches in NFL history to win a playoff game against the Green Bay Packers. He was big, strong, fast, and put up great numbers almost every season of his career. On paper, he was the kind of player that any coach should have wanted on his team. Except there was one problem: no one wanted him, because more often than not he would ruin the chemistry of his team by being a hater.

Despite having all of the talent in the world, TO was known for being selfish and caring more about himself than his team. If he didn't get the ball enough, he was unhappy, and he made sure everyone knew it.

Throughout his career, TO was a seed of negativity that inevitably grew until it consumed the team and doomed its season. Sure, he was a great competitor at heart—that's how he made his legendary catch—but by the end of his career, while he was still good enough to play, no one wanted him because of his pervasively negative and selfish attitude.

A TO isn't necessarily a person incapable of playing your games, it's just someone whose attitude could potentially undermine a team or your momentum.

When you start your games, or perhaps as they play out, you might notice that one or more of the players is a TO, with a hater complex. Maybe they don't want to play a certain game at all, maybe they won't cooperate with their teammates, or maybe they just won't stop complaining.

First thing to do, and this might seem counterintuitive to logic, not to mention difficult, is to **completely ignore the TO**. I know how hard it can be to do this to a person, and you might feel guilty, but it's the most effective and efficient course of action you can take. It works.

Instead of worrying about the TO, put all of your focus on creating momentum with the players who are having fun and participating already. If you slow things down for a TO, you risk alienating the other players who've already bought into the game. Instead, embrace them.

Once you get your momentum going, you can then use the TO as a silent gauge for your success. Hopefully, with the game moving along, the TO will see all the fun everyone is having and won't be able to resist joining in, or at least toning down his attitude in order to fit in better.

If that doesn't happen, don't give up on the TO just yet. This player works for you, so you must know a bit about him. You've undoubtedly had conversations with him, and as a leader you've tried to figure out what motivates him. Try adding something new to the game that you think will inspire the TO specifically, e.g. if you know he loves getting time off on the weekend, make a prize a three-day weekend, and see if he bites.

If either of the above scenarios plays out, then you've won by achieving the best outcome possible with a TO. You might have to re-motivate him in the future, but you now know you can do it.

In the event you're unsuccessful in winning the TO over, don't worry. In most cases, he will realize the games aren't going away, and he'll either move on naturally or cave and buy in.

Whatever you do, try to avoid issuing any kind of ultimatum. Don't engage him in a "you have to do this" type talk, or try to pressure him any other way. Most people take an ultimatum as a threat. They take it personally, and it only further antagonizes them toward you. Even if they do end up doing what you want, they'll probably feel bitter and resentful about it.

Laying down an ultimatum should *only* be a last resort and *only* if you're willing to fire the employee if he is still unwilling to cooperate. Don't make empty threats if you can't afford to follow through.

The one exception to how to deal with a TO is when you feel like an entire team is full of them. In this instance, the game can't even build momentum. This has happened to me, and although it's not common, it might happen to you, and when it does, it can make for a long, tiring day or week at the office.

If this happens, you need to do two things: First, rethink your prizes.

You need a prize so big that no one can ignore it. This might cost more than you want to spend at the time, but look at it as an investment.

For example: maybe your team plays fantasy football and it's the middle of football season. Go out and buy a seventy-inch TV as a prize. Or maybe it's the middle of winter, and your city has been frigid, pummeled with bad weather for the last month. A four-day trip to the Bahamas could do the trick.

Whatever you choose for a prize, make sure it's one a person would have to be crazy not to want.

After you have this prize, show it to the players immediately.

Call them around and make a scene of it. Set it in a place where your employees will see it every day. The more they have to see it the better. It should be obvious how to display a TV, but even if it's something like a trip to the Bahamas, all you have to do is get a big cardboard cut-out of a person on the beach, and add a sign that says something like "All expenses paid trip to the Bahamas" or "This could be you."

Make it visual and undeniable. **Show and tell.**

The second part of your strategy is to secretly enlist one of the players as a mole to help you by giving you private feedback on the other players.

Employees are much more comfortable talking openly to each other than to their boss. Pick the most influential or natural leader out of the bunch. You want someone who likes control, and wants to do things his own way. Often, you'll find this is the most outspoken or most persuasive member of the group.

You can have a simple chat with the potential mole in your office, or you could invite him out to lunch, or for an after work drink. Keep it professional, of course, but the key is make sure he knows he's been singled out for a special role. You tell him you want to include him in running the games and picking the payout and prizes. Or that you want him to handle the money.

Whatever you do, you're playing off his desire for control. Only once he accepts the offer do you tell him you want him to be a mole. If he turns down it down, find someone else.

This works in two ways. Either this player has enough influence to get the others on board, or he'll feed you the information you need to get them on board, whether that involves changing the way the games are set up, the teams arranged, or the prizes offered.

Stick with these approaches, and eventually you will get the team moving and/or overcome the presence of a TO. It isn't always easy to do at first, but I have never failed or witnessed anyone else fail to do so.

2. HESITATORS

When you first start your games, you might encounter a TO who doesn't want to play. But there is second kind of player who might not want to, and that's the wallflower.

This person isn't a hater. In fact, he doesn't even have to be a hesitator by the most literal definition of the term. But typically this is a person who for whatever reason, shyness, doubt, fear, or anxiety, is reluctant to play, or if they do play, to commit fully.

It doesn't matter that everyone else is having fun, this player, because of his own neuroses or whatever other reason, simply can't help participating with only the minimal contribution necessary.

This is a problem you need to deal with, and you can't just ignore this person like you would a TO.

Let's pretend the team is an improv troupe. The fundamental key to improv isn't natural comedy chops, looks, wit, or intelligence; it's commitment. On a good improv team, everyone goes all-in on every character, choice, and emotion. When they're happy, they laugh loudly, when they're sad, tears roll down their cheeks, and when they're angry, they turn red as turnips and yell. You laugh because they're so committed to the scene and confident in that commitment. When someone is hesitant, you notice it as an audience member, and the scene loses its magic.

You don't want your game to lose its magic, its hold over the players, so you need to help the hesitators commit.

You do this by using alter-egos.

When I was a kid, my favorite TV show was *Emergency*. It was close to my heart because my hero was my grandfather, and he was a fireman. Every night I would turn my bed into a fire engine and pretend I was Roy and Johnny was my partner, as we raced to save helpless citizens from burning buildings.

As a kid I didn't think about it beforehand, but this is called creating an alter-ego. And this is the best way to overcome hesitation. If you asked me to reenact a fire rescue today, the first thing I'd do is pretend that I'm Roy DeSoto all over again.

Everyone has a childhood hero. I'm not necessarily talking about a parent or grandparent, but super heroes, movie characters, policemen, firemen, singers, dancers, celebrities, etc.

Alter-egos, or aliases, work for hesitators because they allow a person to pretend he's someone who wouldn't hesitate.

Think of Clark Kent and Superman. Sure, all he does is take off his glasses and don a caped uniform, but Superman is diametrically opposite Clark as a person. Clark is shy, reserved, and meek. Superman is bold, active, and powerful.

In taking on a new persona with its own voice and personality, a person no longer has to be himself. An alter-ego allows a hesitator to act in ways he never would have otherwise, because he doesn't have to deal with the anxiety of acting a certain way as himself. In improv this is playing a character. In a game in the office, it can be the same thing.

You can incorporate alter-egos into your games by having players use nicknames. Maybe a simple nickname is enough to get a player to overcome hesitation. If it's not, encourage the players to create character traits for these nicknames. Maybe Chet, the quiet sandwich artist, becomes Pete, a smooth talking cad who knows his way around a sandwich as well as he does a woman. And maybe Julie, too cool for school cashier, becomes Veronica, a confident, take no prisoners woman looking to win at all costs.

You might not want players interacting with customers as crazy characters, though I'm not saying that that wouldn't be fun or work, but even if they just play these characters behind closed doors, the personas will bring out new sides of their selves, and compel them to be more competitive, talkative, and engaged players.

The same strategy applies to teams.

By having players choose a team name, you make the team more of a tangible entity, something they are really a part of. Instead of being on this or that team, a player is on the *Sandwich Picassos*, or the *Combo Kings*, etc.

Working together to come up with a team name will bring the players closer, as will making up a persona for the team, brainstorming ideas and characters or roles they want to play on it. This fosters camaraderie, and the closer a team gets at the beginning, the more likely they will be to encourage and push each other, patting each other on the back for wins, and picking each other up in losses.

Through alter-egos, you give players a way to overcome hesitation. This will work, although to what degree depends on the person. Regardless, it's your best approach to dealing with hesitators, and the surest way to see a performance boost from them.

3. CHEATERS

Everyone has heard stories about what happens to cheaters in Las Vegas. From blacklists, to bruises and broken limbs, to shallow desert graves, Casinos have an infamous way of dealing with cheaters. But what do you do if someone cheats at one of your games?

Obviously you can't act like a casino. And these days, casinos tend to lean more towards blacklisting a cheater than roughing him up anyway. With lawsuits and YouTube, no casino wants to risk getting caught doing something on camera, after all. So what do you do if someone cheats?

Fire the cheater immediately.

Depending on the situation, this could be easy or one of the most difficult things you've ever had to do. But it doesn't matter what the reason is for a person to cheat; if it happens even once, you must fire him right on the spot. I don't care if he was stealing money to donate to cancer research. You have to fire him. Otherwise, the moment the integrity of your games is compromised, you risk losing your players' faith, your momentum, and your ability to use games at all.

"But what if no one gets hurt?" you might be saying. "What the cheating is necessary?"

I'm reminded of something I read in the book *Freakonomics*. There was a part about teachers changing students test answers and attempting to inflate their scores, because if scores didn't go up, the school would lose funding and teachers would lose jobs.[10]

Sure, the inflations worked at first. But eventually people outside the school noticed that the score increases were too great. They looked into them further and grew suspicious. The next time the tests were given out, more stringent rules were applied, and this time, without the aid of cheating, the students' scores plummeted. The gains from cheating had been short term, and the issues plaguing the school were exposed once again.

Even if things hadn't worked out this way, and the cheating had continued, it was only a mask for the problem, not a solution. Inevitably, cheating would've come back to haunt someone, somehow, whether that's a student who grows up thinking cheating is the best way to get ahead, or a school that not only loses funding but also its whole charter, because of a scandal.

The only way to stop cheating is to do so immediately. Nip that weed in the bud, and move forward.

4. LOSERS

At the end of most games, one team or player will win, and everyone else will lose. That's just how a competitive game works.

These days, too often people give out last place trophies or participation awards so that no one feels left out or bad. But that goes against the spirit of competition. The whole point of having a game that can be won is that it *can be won*. That's what incentivizes a player to work harder. To win. If everyone won, what would be the point of playing to win?

That's not to say everyone doesn't get a prize. By giving out spiffs, you ensure that no one, barring a complete lack of acceptable performance, walks away without something. But someone needs to win.

Too often I've gone back to businesses to check on their games and found that players have lost interest. I asked why, and the boss tells me that they don't try because they're used to getting the prize no matter what. As it turns out, these bosses feel bad when their employees work so hard and lose, so they give them the prize anyway. This is a huge mistake.

Yes, it's hard to see the disappointment on players' faces after a loss, to watch them walk away empty-handed following a valiant effort, but the second you bend the rules, you compromise the power of Gamification.

Trust me, when a team works hard and loses, more often than not, they will come back for the next game and work even harder.

It's possible you'll encounter sore losers at times, but if variations in games and prizes aren't enough to reinvigorate them, I know a few other tactics that do the trick.

You could rearrange the teams. Maybe this will make things seem fairer, especially if the previous game ended in a blow out. But if the last game was close, you could keep the team together and give them a chance to win all or a part of what they lost in the last game back.

Put the new day's carrot slightly above the previous day's performance. If they sold seven of something the previous day and lost, offer them the previous day's lost prize if they sell ten, or beat the prior winning team's number. And while this might take an investment on your part, by setting up the new prize as a higher sales number, you can help absorb its cost.

For fairness, you should make this prize open to all teams. But wait. Then that puts the losing team right back behind the eight ball, doesn't it?

Not so much.

Harvard studied 60,000 basketball games, including 18,000 NBA games, and found that teams who were down by one point at halftime were more likely to win than teams that were ahead by one point at halftime. If you look at the chart below, you'll see that even a team down by eight at halftime still has a better than thirty percent chance of winning.[11]

Being behind by a small total can be a powerful motivator for a team. If you set up a situation that lets the team feel like they are close enough to win, their natural, human competitiveness will make them work harder to reach the number, even though they previously failed to do so. If they were good enough to keep it close last time, they should be good enough to win. Even if they lose again, at least you gave them a second chance. And when you start a new game, they'll be all the more hungrier.

5. THE HANGOVER

Someone once said, "I feel sorry for people who don't drink, because when they wake up in the morning, that's the best they're going to feel all day."

Depending on the source, this quote's usually attributed to Frank Sinatra, Dean Martin, or Jack Lemmon. But regardless of who said it, there's an underlying truth in it that goes beyond drinking. Sometimes when you live life to the fullest, you wake up feeling the pain.

An alcohol hangover is a miserable experience. The receptors in your brain are damaged. It's like a tiny jackhammer is pounding inside your brain. You're dehydrated and achy. You feel slow and anxious. Getting out of bed seems like a chore, and all you want is to eat something greasy and then sleep until the pain is gone. While the physical symptoms might differ, that same listless, motivation-deprived hangover inevitably follows any experience that involves an exertion of effort, either physical or mental.

Gamification is a system that's designed to help you get the most out of your employees. When you have it working, your business will have momentum unlike any it's ever had before. But that momentum comes through the efforts of your employees, and inevitably, it's going to lead to a hangover.

I was with a group of business leaders a few months ago, and it just so happened that the creator of Space X Challenge had started a new site (X Prize) for business to Gamify solutions that they needed help with, and his partner was there speaking.

The topic was using Gamification to build tribes and solve business problems by challenging freelance engineers, programmers, or hobbyists with prizes.

He put on a clinic.

The perfect example of this is offering a $10 Million dollar prize for the Space X Challenge. He inspired 26 private teams from around the world to build the best spaceship. This move was expensive, but so far it's led to major progress in an innovative space program that seems like our country's best bet to fill the void left by NASA. I realized quickly that what he's done and continues to do using Gamification is nothing short of genius.
During the group after-discussion, I brought up how I had been

using Gamification. I discussed my results from using it, gaming software I had developed, and also mentioned that I was writing a book on the topic (which you're reading right now).

Next thing I knew, this conversation had carried over into dinner, and later to the bar.

Over drinks, I found myself answering questions and explaining different strategies I'd found successful, when one of the guys at the table said, "You know playing games with employees in a business setting only works for a couple months, and then it loses its impact."

I quickly replied, "Yeah, we call that The Hangover."

His head jerked back so quickly I thought he gave himself whiplash.

"You have a term for that?" he blurted out.

"Of course. It's an inevitable aspect of Gamification."

As Gamification gives your business momentum, you'll reach a point where everything is going so well that you might start thinking you're impervious to the hangover. But I promise it's coming. This isn't an "if," but a "when."

It could take a few weeks or months to hit, but eventually you'll run into a wall where you will feel like the games don't work anymore, and no matter what you try, your feet are mired in quicksand.

This is going to happen. Accept it. And be ready to overcome it.

Whenever I have a hangover after a night of drinking, people always tell me to have another drink. They call it having "Hair of the dog that bit you last night."

It's odd to think that what causes the sickness helps cure it, but I distinctly remember that it worked every time.

When the hangover hits your business, this same logic applies. First, acknowledge it. Then figure out what caused it.

The most common cause is that the games have become habit, and the problems and distractions of the outside world are no longer masked by the newness and fun of the games. I hinted at this earlier when discussing how you need to vary your games and prizes to keep up with twitch speed.

The second most common cause is that the players are exhausted.

This comes most often with a very competitive team that can't stand to lose, and that literally exhausts themselves trying to win. Most often this happens right after a big month-end push, or a record week/month of sales. Otherwise, the exhaustion could come from some fighting/hostility that has come up from the competition.

Whatever the reason, your employees mentally and physically just can't get the fight back. You need a pattern interrupt.

The pattern interrupt could be as simple as changing the venue of the games from your office to a player's desk, or switching from team games to individual games, or vice versa. Or you could shuffle players around on teams.

If the hangover has come from games turning into habit, then switching things up might do the trick to get the teams going again. If it doesn't, then you need to up the stakes and the intensity. You need to challenge them. Come up with a bigger goal. If before you wanted better than 60% sales on combos, now you want better than 75%. And with a bigger goal, comes a bigger prize.

On the flipside, if the previous goal was something big and the players are exhausted, make the new goal smaller. If your games mostly focus on rewarding sales, perhaps change the focus for a couple of days to something easier and more fun, like positive customer comments or feedback. By lessening the pressure and mental work, you give them a chance to get some easy wins based more on fun and less on performance. These wins will boost confidence, and that helps replenish energy.

During this easier period, lower the game payout and build up a war chest. Then when within as little as a few days you notice they've got their edge back, use the prize money you've saved up to offer something they can't resist: a new grand prize, double payouts, whatever you want.

It's not rocket science to overcome the hangover, but the secret is not to quit or get demotivated when it comes. Just acknowledge it to yourself and switch things up.

ONE MORE PROBLEM

There is one more potential problem that you need to be ready for as you Gamify your business…

You.

At the end of the day, this is a system fueled by your employees but run by you. While it will improve morale and make your workplace exciting and fun, the point of this system is to increase your income and help you reach your business goals. And in order for Gamification to work, you have to be ready and willing to take all responsibility for it and its outcomes.

SHORTCUTS

To begin with, you have to make sure to cover all of your bases. These games are very intuitive and you might be tempted to take a shortcut to getting them up and running.
Don't do that. These games are going to work, but you need to

take your time and think things through. As you come up with your goals, do whatever research you can. Survey the market, analyze past performance, and project future costs (you should've been doing all of this already).

As you develop your games, try to anticipate anything that could possibly happen. You don't have to be psychic, and things might and likely will happen that you couldn't have predicted, but if you start from a position of at least aiming to predict them, you'll be more mentally prepared to make any necessary changes.

Lastly, before you start your games, be as clear as possible about the rules and prize structure. These games are going to be the backbone of your momentum moving forward, and you need everyone involved to fully understand them. Write down as much as you can and make sure that your employees see and have access to the rules.

TRACKING

I'm not an attorney. I've Gamified businesses in almost every state in the country, and am certain you will have little to no problem doing so with yours, but before you get things going, you should check with your labor attorney about any legal *t*'s you need to cross or *i*'s you need to dot.

I touched on this earlier, but any prizes of monetary value that your employees win will qualify as income, and they will need to pay taxes on them.

This might seem unfair, but it's how our country's tax system works. It's no different than when a person wins the lottery or on a game show like *The Price Is Right*. The winner has to pay taxes on his winnings just like your employees. The only difference is that this is your business, and if you don't make it clear that they need to pay taxes, you could potentially find yourself in a compromised position legally.

This really is easy to avoid, though. If you can, talk to a labor attorney. Then make sure you tell your employees that they will have to pay taxes on all winnings of monetary value. Write this down for them to see. Track the costs of whatever anyone wins and submit these totals to your payroll department if you have one, or else account for them yourself. Report this money as earnings for your employees. Again, I would advise you talk to a labor attorney to make sure of how your state's labor and tax laws apply to your games, but if you do the basics above, you should be covered legally.

GREED

As Gamification creates momentum in your business, and you start noticing the increase in your revenue, and/or other goals being met, you might be tempted to push things further, even beyond obvious or legal limits.

Do not do this.

I can't stress how important it is to avoid the temptations of greed. Gamification works, and you're very likely going to find you and your business soaring to higher limits than ever before. But you must keep everything on the level and legal. It would be an utter shame if upon sniffing success, you undermined yourself because of greed.

In telling you how to use this system, I'm also assuming that you have business and moral ethics, as well as a legitimate product or enterprise. If you're running a pyramid scheme or hoping to use it for any other illicit purpose, then Gamification is not for you. In fact, I would suggest you put this book down and work on getting yourself on a right and legal course before even worrying about Gamifying anything.

CONFIDENCE

Above all, as you use Gamification, doubt is your greatest enemy. I've said it so many times in this book, that these games will create the momentum you and your business need to reach your goals, and you need to believe and have genuine confidence in that. If you don't, you're dooming yourself from the start.

One major cause of doubt is that you might feel like while games have obvious applications in sales environments, or for certain types of employees or workplaces, you question whether they're right for you, your business, and your employees.

Yes, unequivocally yes, they are right for you.

It doesn't matter whether you sell a product, work in city hall, manage wealth, or even sweep streets. Whatever your business is, identify your goal, your MVPs, and these games will work. Bulldog Subs was my example in this book because I thought it would help make the system easy to understand, but by no means is it limited to business with traditional products. Below I've included ten different examples to help convey the many different goals you can use Gamification to achieve.

EXAMPLES

1. Advertising Agency

GOALS:
- Ad placements
- Proposals
- New clients A specific client (a whale)

GAMES:

- Offer daily or weekly spiffs to the players or teams that put together the best proposals. Just as you'll be competing against other agencies, have your teams compete against each other for the right to pitch the clients.
- Offer a big prize or commission to the team that brings in the biggest client during a time period designated by you.

2. Café/Coffee Shop

GOALS:
- Sell more of your MVPs (Combos, gift cards/ memberships, etc.)
- Push a new product

GAMES:
- As with any business, you need to identify your MVPs. At your sandwich shop, this was combos. At a coffee chain, it might be combos as well, or something else. Whatever it is, make it the focus of your game.
- The lesson we took from Starbucks VIA was that even a new product at a chain nearly impervious to failure can benefits greatly from games. Maybe VIA would have succeeded anyway, but Starbucks is an enormous company with nearly unlimited research resources, and they chose to use games to push VIA. Whether you own a Starbucks or your own coffee shop, or simply manage one, whenever you have a new product, games should a major basis of your sales strategy. Customers are going to be unsure about something new, and will feed off the positive energy of your employees.
- If you own a coffee shop, or a chain, your aim is to gain as many customers as possible (obviously), especially repeat customers. One way to do that is through monthly subscriptions or gift cards. Your customers are going to get coffee somewhere, and this a way to compel them to get it from you and to keep doing so. If current Club Price is $20 a month, I would raise it to $25 before starting the games. For gift cards, create a point system. Every card sold earns a team points or tickets they will be able to use toward winning a prize.

3. Car Dealership/Auto Body Shop

GOALS:
- Upsells
- Cars
- MVPs (services offered)
- Alignments, oil changes, rotations, etc.

GAMES:
- Commissions for sales of cars are inherent here, but incentivize upsells. As we did with our example using combos, spiff and reward players for upsells.
- You don't just *want*, you *need* the back end of your dealership, the service center, to pull in steady business. As you've done up front, push your employees to upsell customers. Reward players or teams that sell the most routine maintenance packages.

4. Charity/Philanthropy

GOALS:
- Number of donations
- Size of donations
- New benefactors

GAMES:
- The total number donations received is a good starting place for points in a game here, but I'm guessing your goal leans more toward total money raised. Set up a game structure where smaller prizes like spiffs come from getting donations or new benefactors, while bigger prizes go to those players who bring in the largest donations during each game.
- As with any game, cash prizes work best, but you don't have to monetize your game, and since you run a charity, you very well might not be able to for legal and/or moral reasons. You can use other rewards like trophies or plaques instead. If you have any special events, take time during them to honor the teams or players of the year (or designated time period).
- Find a wealthy benefactor who can match the largest donation a team or player pulls in (or do so yourself if you have the financial means). Knowing that the money they raised has just been doubled could be more rewarding than any prize for a team.

5. Investment Bank

GOALS:
- Bring in new clients
  - A specific client (a whale)
- Levels and size of investments
- Return on investments

GAMES:
- I'm guessing there's a strong chance you already have employees who work extremely long and hard hours in this business, but that doesn't mean they can't have fun. There's a reason the phrase "Live hard, play hard," gets uttered at some point by every young investment banker on Wall Street. Play off this mentality.
- Build your games around the lives these players already live. Obviously your focus is income, and you'll reward teams for new clients, big investments, and returns, but since these players are already working so hard maybe set up a prize based on the team that clocks the most hours in a given week. And when it comes to prizes, money works, but for players working hundred hour weeks, a three day weekend might have more immediate value to a team than anything else.

6. Police Department

GOALS:

- Lower crime rate
- Generate revenue
- Improve community relations
- Increase solve rate

GAMES:

- This is a potentially sticky area, since it involves working for the city or state (or maybe even the Federal Government), but once you make sure you're abiding by the rules and law yourself, you can use games to incentivize your teams. One simple way is through tickets. Yes, people hate tickets, especially petty ones like those for jaywalking and parking. But while these are annoying, they also convey a police presence not only to the people getting the tickets, but also to those who witness it. This will decrease the likelihood of a crime being committed in that area.
- Police can be the backbone of a safe community, but in many areas they are often viewed by the locals with a measure of distance and dislike (in some cases even hatred). Create a game that rewards community outreach and involvement. Spiff (make sure the prizes are legal) employees for spending time giving back to the community, whether that's at a local youth center, shelter, church, or any other place where they can interact with locals and improve your department's image.

7. Real Estate Agency

GOALS:

- New listings
- Offers
- Properties sold/leased

GAMES:

- To sell big in this business, you need big things to sell. Your agents are already going to be getting commissions on sales, but for your real estate business to have momentum, you need as many desirable and potentially profitable listings as you can handle, and them some. I'd build your games around getting new listings, with a reward system that balances the number of listings brought in against the value of each listing. Spiff the basic numbers, but offer bigger prizes for total value.

8. Salon/Barbershop

GOALS:
- Bookings
- Products pushed

GAMES:

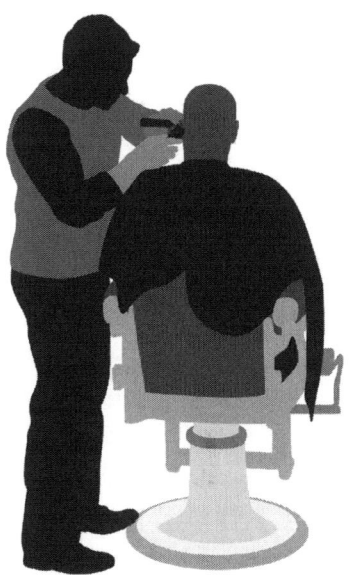

- You want your salon fully booked. To make that happen, you've picked the best location and best staff you could find. But you still need to make sure that a regular roll of clients is coming in. As with any client-centric business, you'll want to reward those teams/ players who bring in the most clients and generate the most revenue. Reward upsells. Make sure to put a colorist on each team, if you do that in your business.

- While a successful salon or barbershop can be a good source or sustainable lifelong income, from what I've seen, the ones that make the leap to the next level and generate the largest profits don't necessarily do so through franchising, but through products. If you don't have a line of products yet, I'd suggest considering creating one. And if you do, build a major part of your game around your employees pushing the products that have your name on them.

9. Sports Team

GOALS:
- Winning championships
- Ticket/concession sales
- Attract blue chip talent

GAMES:

- Especially in this country, when people think of sports, the massive media empire of professional sports comes to mind. But sports span all ages, and your goals are very likely going to be contingent on the team you work with and what your role is. Since the aim of this book is to help businesses, I'm addressing those coaches/leaders who do so for a living (but hey volunteer youth coach, I know you might be out there, and by all means use this advice as you see fit).
- If you follow the NFL, you might recall the scandal involving the New Orleans Saints called "Bountygate." I mentioned it earlier in this book as well. Basically, the coaches offered players cash rewards for physically injuring players on other teams. For doing this, they were fined, players involved were suspended, and the coaches who organized it were suspended for a full season. Obviously rewarding players for injuring others is wrong, and I don't care if it's something that other teams in the NFL did. But at the heart of this scandal is a game. And considering that the Saints won the Super Bowl that season, it's safe to say the game worked. So how do you create a game like this that isn't evil? Simple. Look at the Seattle Seahawks. Every week, Pete Carroll sets up a game during practice for his players. It has its own point system, awarding the defense points

for big plays like interceptions and sacks, and the offense similar points for scoring, etc. If you're familiar with fantasy football, think of it as a real life adaptation. There's no intention to injure anyone involved in these games. And there aren't even prizes. But all you have to do is look at the Seahawks' 2014 Lombardi Trophy to see how well it works. Using a game like this can make your practices fun and your team a winner!

- Other games you can play could reward performance. College football teams often do this with helmet stickers, but you can use any reward you want (just make sure you stay within the rules of your league, which might outlaw cash and certain prizes). Since certain players are naturally going to dominate performance-wise, make sure you set up a system that has balance. If it's baseball, maybe you say you'll get the player with the highest on base percentage for the week (we're not saying batting average here since it's not 1950 anymore) a gift card to his favorite restaurant. Likewise, you reward the player that shows the most hustle or team spirit (players on the bench are often essential to a teams' morale).

- If you own or run a sports team, you're looking to increase revenue and attract high value players. Set up a reward system of games for your recruiters and employees. Award the team that sells the most souvenirs or combos. Have a prize pool for the recruiter who (legally) lands the most or best blue chip prospects.

***

Those were only nine examples of business using games. I'll get to the tenth in a moment, but what I want you to take away from these examples isn't necessarily the exact application of games, or a guideline to what your goals should be; these examples are representative of different kind of businesses, and how games can be used to meet the goals in all of them. Even if you can't offer cash prizes, or prizes of any monetary value, games still bring immense value to your workplace.

In reality, there are more types of businesses and game applications than I could break down in a book one hundred times the length of this. But rather than require you to sit and read the *War and Peace* of Gamification, I want you to use those examples to extrapolate how to use the games yourself.

As I've said, you are the driving force behind these games. Your moral integrity, vision, drive, and most of all confidence are going to be what dictate the success not only of these games, but of your business. I've worked with all kinds of businesses to implement games, not to mention I've had experience working in many different fields, but while I've learned a lot, and I'm a fast learner, I would hope that you've found yourself in your leadership position because you are or are fast becoming an expert in your field. You know the fundamentals of a game, a goal and a prize, and now you know how to set them up. You can do this. You can achieve the success you want.

Hold on, you're probably thinking. *you said there were ten examples of businesses here, but listed only nine. What's the tenth?*

Can you guess?

I'll give you a hint: it's the most important business venture any person could ever make. This is an enterprise that carries immense risk, potentially life or death, and will not only impact your future, but the future of the whole world.

You got it yet?

I don't care what you do right now, or what you think you can do. Nothing is more important than this business. Think about it.

10. Parenting

Okay, so maybe I cheated a little bit with this last one. Being a parent isn't really a business at all. But if you think about it, you have a goal: to raise your child well and prepare them to have a successful, fulfilling future. Children very well might be a major reason you're reading this book. You want your business to succeed because you want

to provide the best life possible for your family. Even if children aren't in your plans, as a human being you can't deny that they are at least extremely important (unless you would prefer we go extinct as a species). And guess what, Gamification even works with children.

Maybe that's no surprise to you—most people know that children love games and prizes—but it's probably surprising to find this as a final example in a book on how to Gamify businesses.

Using games to incentivize children is nothing new. From offering an allowance based on behavior and chores (spiffs), to rewards for good grades and deeds (pots), to having a day once a year full of grand prizes—I'm talking about birthdays, Christmas, Hanukkah and any other holiday that involves gifts—Gamification is woven into the fabric of parenting. Why do you think Santa's Naughty and Nice Lists exist? They're games.

Yes, some children don't get presents every year. Some don't have the same opportunities as others. But at lest some parts of all childhoods are Gamified. Even grades in school are games. When's the last time you got an A for good performance at work? You get paid. That's always been your reward.

But children haven't been jaded by adulthood. They want money, but they want toys, and As, and fun too. I like to think most of us always retain that spirit, at least somewhere, deep down. Parenting is the most important business in the world, and if Gamification works for that, it will work for you.

NOTES

1. Ben Chang et al., "Job Satisfaction: 2014 Edition." The Conference Board (June 2014), accessed February 9, 2015, https://www.conference-board.org/topics/publicationdetail.cfm?publicationid=2785

2. Susan Adams, "Unhappy Employees Outnumber Happy Ones By Two To One Worldwide." *Forbes* (October 10, 2013), accessed Feb. 9, 2015, http://www.forbes.com/sites/susanadams/2013/10/10/unhappy-employees-outnumber-happy-ones-by-two-to-one-worldwide/

3. Ajay K. Agrawal, John Mchale, and Alex Oettl, "Why Stars Matter" (March 2014): quoted in Drake Baer, "Here's Why Hiring A Star Performer Lifts Up An Entire Organization." *Business Insider* (April 1, 2014), accessed February 11, 2015, http://www.businessinsider.com/hire-stars-because-they-attract-more-stars-says-science-2014-4#ixzz3c8dQOUs8

4. Ibid.

5. "Gartner Says By 2015, More Than 50 Percent of Organizations That Manage Innovation Processes Will Gamify Those Processes," Gartner (April 12, 2011), accessed February 10, 2015, http:www.gartner.com/newsroom/id/1629214

6. Katie Larsen McClarty et al., "A Literature Review of Gaming in Education," Pearson Assessments (June 2012), accessed February 11, 2015, http://researchnetwork.pearson.com/wp-content/uploads/lit_review_of_gaming_in_education.pdf

7. "Gartner Reveals Top Predictions for IT Organizations and Users for 2013 and Beyond," Gartner (October 24, 2012), accessed February 8, 2015, http://www.gartner.com/newsroom/id/2211115

8. Jeffrey Jensen Arnett and Joseph Schwab, "The Clark University Poll of Emerging Adults: Thriving, Struggling & Hopeful," (December 2012): 12, accessed February 13, 2015, https://www.clarku.edu/clark-poll-emerging-adults/pdfs/clark-university-poll-emerging-adults-findings.pdf

9. Herbert Wagner et al., "Individual and Team Performance in Team-Handball: A Review," *Journal of Sports Science & Medicine* 13, no. 4 (December 1, 2014), accessed February 12, 2015, http://www.ncbi.nlm.nih.gov/pmc/articles/PMC4234950/

10. Steven D, Levitt and Stephen J. Dubner, *Freakonomics: a rogue economist explores the hidden side of everything*, (2005), New York: William Morrow.

11. Jonah Berger, "If You Want to Win, Tell Your Team it's Losing (A Little)," *Harvard Business Review* (October 2011), accessed Jan. 5, 2015, https://hbr.org/2011/10/if-you-want-to-win-tell-your-team-its-losing-a-little

REFERENCES

Adams, Susan, "Unhappy Employees Outnumber Happy Ones By Two To One Worldwide." *Forbes*. October 10, 2013. Accessed Feb. 9, 2015. http://www.forbes.com/sites/susanadams/2013/10/10/unhappy-employees-outnumber-happy-ones-by-two-to-one-worldwide/

"Alter Ego." Wikipedia. Accessed Feb. 9, 2015.

Andersen, Janna and Rainie, Lee. "The Future of Gamification." Pew Research Center. May 18, 2012. Accessed Feb. 9, 2015.

Agrawal, Ajay K., John McHale, and Alex Oettl. "Why Stars Matter" (March 2014). Quoted in Drake Baer, "Here's Why Hiring A Star Performer Lifts Up An Entire Organization." *Business Insider*. April 1, 2014. Accessed February 11, 2015, http://www.businessinsider.com/hire-stars-because-they-attract-more-stars-says-science-2014-4#ixzz3c8dQOUs8

Arnett, Jeffrey Jensen, and Joseph Schwab. "The Clark University Poll of Emerging Adults: Thriving, Struggling & Hopeful." December 2012: 12. Accessed February 13, 2015. https://www.clarku.edu/clark-poll-emerging-adults/pdfs/clark-university-poll-emerging-adults-findings.pdf

Berger, Jonah. "If You Want to Win, Tell Your Team it's Losing (A Little)." *Harvard Business Review*. October 2011. Accessed Jan. 5, 2015. https://hbr.org/2011/10/if-you-want-to-win-tell-your-team-its-losing-a-little

Burke, Brian. "How Gamification Motivates the Masses." *Forbes*. April 10, 2014. Accessed Feb. 9, 2015. http://www.forbes.com/sites/gartnergroup/2014/04/10/how-gamification-motivates-the-masses/

Chang, Ben, Michelle Kan, Gad Levanon, and Rebecca L. Ray. "Job Satisfaction: 2014 Edition." The Conference Board (June 2014). Accessed February 9, 2015. https://www.conference-board.org/topics/publicationdetail.cfm?publicationid=2785

Cosier, Susan. "Why We Gamble: The Enticement of Almost Winning." *LiveScience*. Feb. 5, 2010. Accessed Feb. 9, 2015.

Ellin, Abby. "The Beat (Up) Generation." *Psychology Today*. March 20, 2014. Accessed Feb. 11, 2015.

"Gamification: Extrinsic and Intrinsic Motivators." Enterprise Gamification. Retrieved October 7, 2014.

"Gartner Reveals Top Predictions for IT Organizations and Users for 2013 and Beyond." Gartner. October 24, 2012. Accessed February 8, 2015. http://www.gartner.com/newsroom/id/2211115

"Gartner Says By 2015, More Than 50 Percent of Organizations That Manage Innovation Processes Will Gamify Those Processes." Gartner. April 12, 2011. Accessed February 10, 2015. http:www.gartner.com/newsroom/id/1629214

Hamari, J. and Koivisto, J. "Social Motivations to Use Gamification: An Empirical Study of Gamifying Exercise." 2013. *Proceedings of the 21st European Conference on Information Systems, Utrecht, Netherlands, June 5–8.*

Hamari, J., Koivisto, J. and Sarsa, H. "Does Gamification Work? – A Literature Review of Empirical Studies on Gamification." 2014.

Proceedings of the 47th Hawaii International Conference on System Sciences, Hawaii, USA, January 6–9.

Herger, Mario. "Gamification Facts & Figures." Enterprise-Gamification.com.

"How to Create an Alter Ego." WikiHow. Accessed Feb. 10, 2015.

Jabr, Farris. "How the Brain Gets Addicted to Gambling." *Scientific American*, a division of Nature America, Inc. Nov. 1, 2013. Accessed Feb. 10, 2015.

Lee, Kevan. "The Science of Motivation: Your Brain on Dopamine." IDoneThis.Com. Dec. 16, 2013. Accessed Feb. 9, 2015.

Levitt, Steven D., and Stephen J. Dubner. *Freakonomics: a rogue economist explores the hidden side of everything*. New York: William Morrow (2005).

Llopis, Glenn. "10 Ways to Inspire Your Team." *Forbes*. May 6, 2013. Accessed Feb. 8, 2015.

Mangels, John. "Gambling Addicts Arise from Mix of Flawed Thinking, Brain Chemistry, and Habitual Behavior." *The Plain Dealer*, as referenced on: http://blog.cleveland.com/metro/2011/05/gambling_addicts_arise_from_mi.html. May 15, 2011. Accessed Feb. 11, 2015.

McClarty, Katie Larsen, Aline Orr, Peter M. Frey, Robert P Dolan, Victoria Vassileva, Aaron McVay. "A Literature Review of Gaming in Education." Pearson Assessments. June 2012. Accessed February 11, 2015. http://researchnetwork.pearson.com/wp-content/uploads/lit_review_of_gaming_in_education.pdf

Prensky, Marc. "Twitch Speed: Reaching Younger Workers Who Think Differently." *Across the Board Magazine*, Jan 1998. Accessed online Feb. 11, 2015.

"Study: Gambling Affects Brain Like Drugs." ABC News. May 25 (n.d). Accessed Feb. 9, 2015.

Tauer, J. M., & Harackiewicz, J. M. (2003). "The Effects of Cooperation and Competition on Intrinsic Motivation and Performance." *Interpersonal Relations and Group Processes*, n. journal, 849-861. Retrieved from http://psych.wisc.edu/cmsdocuments/TauerHarackiewicz04.pdf

Wagner, Herbert, Thomas Finkenzeller, Sabine Würth and Serge P. von Duvillard. "Individual and Team Performance in Team-Handball: A Review." *Journal of Sports Science & Medicine* 13, no. 4. December 1, 2014. Accessed February 12, 2015. http://www.ncbi.nlm.nih.gov/pmc/articles/PMC4234950/

Willis, Judy. "A Neurologist Makes a Case for the Video Game Model as a Learning Tool." Edutopia.org. April 14, 2011. Accessed Feb. 9, 2015.

Winfrey, Graham. "Why Gamification Works (And How to Do it)". Inc (website). Accessed Feb. 10, 2015.

16106918R00100

Printed in Great Britain
by Amazon